Where is a great place to find 1,000 Facts & Figures
about Yellowstone National Park? Here!

YELLOWSTONE
TRIVIA

Including Crossword Puzzles, Quote Quests™, Word Games & MORE

Written by
Janet Spencer, Trivia Queen
ROYAL RULER OF USELESS INFORMATION
MASTER OF ARCANE KNOWLEDGE AND EXTRANEOUS LORE
KEEPER OF FORGOTTEN FACTS & STARTLING STATISTICS

Drawings by
Vince Moravek

RIVERBEND PUBLISHING

Dedication

Thanks first of all to Jerry, for walking next to me for a quarter century, and for keeping the dishes washed while I created this book. Thanks to my publisher Chris for actually listening to my wacky ideas- every writer's dream-come-true! Much appreciation to Vince for the many hours of dedicated drawing. Blessings upon Lee Whittlesey for patient responses to many, many questions, and to the wonderful librarians at Lewis and Clark Library who kept shoving the right books in my direction. Hi Mom! Hey Dad! I'm an author *too!*

Copyright © 2006 by Janet Spencer

Published by Riverbend Publishing, Helena, Montana

Printed in the United States of America

All rights reserved. Reprint rights freely given with prior permission of the publisher.

Cover design by Bob Smith
Text design by Janet Spencer

ISBN: 1-931832-70-6
ISBN 13: 978-1-931832-70-0

Cataloging-in-Publication data is on file at the Library of Congress

Riverbend Publishing
P.O. Box 5833
Helena, MT 59604
1-866-787-2363
www.RiverbendPublishing.com

Contents

GEOGRAPHY

Q. At 2.2 million acres, Yellowstone National Park is larger than the states of Rhode Island and Delaware combined. It's 54 miles east to west and 63 miles north to south. It's the 8th largest national park in the nation. What is America's biggest national park?

A. *Wrangell-St. Elias National Park in Alaska is six times bigger than Yellowstone. Greenland National Park is the largest in the world and it is about 77 times bigger than Yellowstone.*

Q. The Greater Yellowstone Ecosystem encompasses not only Yellowstone but also Grand Teton National Park, two wildlife refuges, parts of six national forests, and various other public and private lands. At 18 million acres, is the Greater Yellowstone Ecosystem larger than, smaller than, or equal to the size of South Carolina?

A. *It is slightly smaller than South Carolina and slightly larger than West Virginia.*

Q. Overall, what is the average elevation of Yellowstone?

A. *About 8,000 feet. By comparison, the average elevation of Montana is 3,400 feet (the lowest of all the Rocky Mountain states) while the average elevation of Colorado is 6,800 feet (the highest of all the Rocky Mountain states).*

Q. The highest temperature ever recorded in Wyoming was 114°F. The highest recorded temperature in Montana was 117°F. What's the record high for Yellowstone?
A) 110°F.   B) 98°F.   C) 82°F.

A. *B) 98°F., set in Lamar Valley in 1936. The record low temperature for Yellowstone is 66° below zero, set in February 1933 at Madison near West Yellowstone.*

Yellowstone is exactly halfway between the Equator and the North Pole.

Q. In spring when snow is melting and rain is falling, 64,000 gallons of water go over the Upper and Lower Falls of the Yellowstone every second. What's the average flow per second in January when the area is under ice and snow?
A) 5,000 GAL.   B) 25,000 GAL.   C) 42,000 GAL.

A. *A) 5,000 gallons per second.*

Q. Lower Falls of the Yellowstone is the tallest waterfall in the park at 308 feet. Is that greater than, lesser than, or equal to the height of the Statue of Liberty as measured from the bottom of the pedestal to the tip of the torch?

A. *About equal to. The statue is 305 feet.*

Q. A huge boulder was once perched on the lip of Tower Fall, looking as if it would tumble over the brink at any moment. In 1871 members of the Hayden Expedition took bets on whether the boulder would fall before, during, or after their dinner. How long before the boulder fell?
A) 1 YEAR   B) 16 YEARS   C) 115 YEARS

A. *C) The boulder fell in 1986, 115 years later, as a natural result of erosion. Whoever said it would fall "after dinner" won the bet.*

Q. What percent of Yellowstone's surface area is water?
A) 5 PERCENT   B) 15 PERCENT   C) 25 PERCENT

A. *C) Five percent, totaling 177 square miles. Yellowstone Lake makes up the majority at 136 square miles.*

Q. Yellowstone River is the longest free-flowing river in the Lower 48 states. It narrowly avoided being dammed in the 1960s, which would have flooded much of the Paradise Valley just north of the park. How long is the river?
A) 124 MILES   B) 398 MILES   C) 670 MILES

A. *C) 670 miles. It flows into the Missouri River near Williston, North Dakota.*

Yellowstone Lake has about 140 tributaries.

Q. The Snake River is the nation's fourth largest river. Its first 42 miles are in Yellowstone. How many dams does the Snake River have along its 1,036-mile length?

  A) 6   B) 25   C) 42

A. *B) 25, which averages out to one dam every 41 miles.*

Q. Shoshone Lake is the largest lake in the contiguous 48 states which completely lacks this significant feature:

  A) FISH   B) ALGAE   C) ROAD

A. *C) A road. It can be reached only by boat or trail.*

Q. Yellowstone Lake holds about four billion gallons of water. That's enough to serve the annual needs of a town whose population is:

  A) 20,000   B) 235,000   C) 750,000

A. *B) 235,000, about the size of Akron, Ohio, or Baton Rouge, Louisiana.*

Q. At the rate that new water enters Yellowstone Lake and old water flows out, how long does it take for all the water in Yellowstone Lake to be completely replaced?

  A) 1 YEAR   B) 10 YEARS   C) 100 YEARS

A. *B) Ten years, as estimated by researchers.*

Q. Yellowstone Lake has a surface area of 136 square miles. It's about 20 miles long and 14 miles wide. Is its surface area greater than, lesser than, or equal to the size of the city limits of Washington, D.C.?

A. *Greater than. It's almost twice as big as the 69 square miles in Washington, D.C.*

Yellowstone Lake sits at an elevation of 7,733 feet above sea level, making it the largest high-elevation lake in North America.

The Shoshone River was originally called the Stinking River.

Q. The average depth of Yellowstone Lake is about 140 feet but the maximum depth is 390 feet. If the Washington Monument were submerged in the deepest part of the lake, would any of it show above the water?

A. *Yes, the top third of the Washington Monument would show above the water. The monument is 555 feet tall.*

> **The only lakes in national parks that are deeper than Yellowstone Lake are Crater Lake in Oregon (1,932 feet) and the waters of Lake Superior off the shore of Isle Royale in Michigan (1,333 feet).**

Q. What percent of the shoreline of Yellowstone Lake is accessible by car?

A. *25 percent, the rest is accessible by boat or trail.*

Q. Although boating is permitted on many lakes in Yellowstone, name the only place where boating on a river is allowed.

A. *Only on the Lewis River between Lewis Lake and Shoshone Lake, and limited to self-propelled boats only. All other rivers are closed to boating to protect wildlife.*

Q. Yellowstone produces 3.3 million acre-feet of water every year, making it one of the richest sources for water in the western United States. Because a single acre-foot is enough to serve the needs of a typical family of four, that's enough to supply the needs of how many people?

    A) 6 MILLION   B) 13 MILLION   C) 27 MILLION

A. *B) 13 million, which is about the population of the state of Illinois.*

Precipitation in the park varies from 8 to 12 inches a year near Gardiner...

Q. The four trillion gallons of water that pour out of Yellowstone each year would be enough to fill Lake Superior how many times?
   A) 3 TIMES   B) 12 TIMES   C) 25 TIMES
A. *B) 12 times.*

Q. How many major rivers originate in the Greater Yellowstone area?
A. *Twelve, including four very large ones: the Snake River, the Missouri River, the Yellowstone River, and the Green River.*

Q. True or False: The headwaters of the Yellowstone River are in Yellowstone.
A. *False. Actually the Yellowstone River originates south of Yellowstone in the Shoshone Mountain Range of Wyoming, flows north into the park and into Yellowstone Lake, and leaves the park at Gardiner, Montana.*

Q. How many waterfalls are in the park?
   A) 17   B) 142   C) 340
A. *C) 340, including over 290 that were recently discovered.*

Q. What percent of Yellowstone's water ends up in the Atlantic Ocean?
   A) 25 PERCENT   B) 50 PERCENT   C) 75 PERCENT
A. *C) 75 percent goes into the Atlantic Ocean and 25 percent goes into the Pacific Ocean.*

> **Yellowstone Lake's 136 square miles of winter ice makes it one of the biggest ice sheets in the continental U.S. In winter when ice is two feet thick on the lake's surface, spots on the bottom of the lake are near boiling from thermal activity.**

... to more than 70 inches of precipitation annually in the southwest corner.

Q. Two Ocean Creek just south of the park splits in half in the middle of a meadow, with one half of the creek running into the Yellowstone River and going down the eastern side of the Continental Divide into the Gulf of Mexico, and the other half running into the Snake River on the west side, ending up in the Pacific Ocean. One is called Atlantic Creek; the other is called Pacific Creek. How many other places are there where a single creek drains into two oceans?

A) NONE   B) THREE   C) SEVEN

A. *None.*

Q. Just west of Yellowstone Lake, Isa Lake, short for Isabel, is a marshy pond. What unusual feature sets this lake apart from all others?

A. *Isa Lake drains to both the Atlantic and the Pacific Ocean. In addition, the* east *side of Isa Lake drains to the* Pacific *and the* west *side drains to the* Atlantic, *backwards of what you would expect.*

Q. There are more than 500 streams and rivers in the park, totaling 2,650 miles. Is that greater than, lesser than, or equal to the distance from Los Angeles to New York City?

A. *About equal to.*

Q. How many of the 2,650 miles of rivers and streams in the park are fishable?

A) 200   B) 675   C) 1,940

A. *A) Only 200 miles. The rest of the waterways are blocked by barriers such as waterfalls, or their temperatures or chemistries will not support fish.*

Indians named the Yellowstone River due to the color of sandstone bluffs...

Q. Of the approximately 200 lakes in Yellowstone, how many have fish in them?

A) 192   B) 97   C) 45

A. *C) 45. The others are too small, too shallow, too hot, too alkali, too acidic, or have access blocked by waterfalls.*

> **Twin Lakes near Norris Geyser Basin are two lakes connected by a small inlet. One is blue; the other is green. One is cooler and one is hotter, so their varied kinds of algae make them different colors. In autumn, one freezes before the other. Twin Lakes, joined like Siamese twins, are very different.**

Q. Bison love to graze in Hayden Valley because the grass is so lush. No trees grow in the valley. Why not?

A) SOIL pH IS WRONG

B) WINTERS TOO HARSH

C) NO GROUNDWATER DRAINAGE

A. *C) No drainage. Hayden Valley was once covered by an arm of Yellowstone Lake. The lake bottom was covered with layer upon layer of clay, silt, sand, and then glacial gravel of all sizes. This mixture plugged up all the porous places. The valley floor is so solidly paved with this mixture that rainwater and snowmelt cannot percolate downward and drain away. The result is mile upon mile of damp lands where sagebrush and grasses grow but trees can't take root.*

Q. How long can a sagebrush plant live?

A. *200 years.*

...that border the river some 300 miles downstream from the park.

Q. The average year-round temperature of Montana is 44.6°F. The average year-round temperature of New York City is 54°F. What is the average year-round temperature of Yellowstone?

    A) 25°F.   B) 35°F.   C) 45°F.

A. *B) 35°F. Some researchers theorize that a three-degree drop in the average temperature would result in a new glacial age for the park.*

Yellowstone can have below-freezing temperatures any month of the year. May has an average of 19 days with temperatures below freezing. In June there are six days; two in July; four in August; and 14 in September. Generally, six months of the year will find the temperatures below freezing on virtually 100 percent of the days.

Q. The lowest point in the park is a little over 5,282 feet at Reese Creek, near the northern entrance. Is that the lowest point in Wyoming?

A. *No, the lowest point in Wyoming is 3,099 feet at Belle Fourche River.*

Q. Eagle Peak at 11,358 feet is the highest point in the park. Is that also the highest point in Wyoming?

A. *No, Wyoming's 13,804-foot Gannett Peak in the Wind River Range is higher.*

The coldest month is January with an average temp of 10.7°F. at Mammoth.

Q. Name the five national forests that surround Yellowstone.

A. *Gallatin and Custer in Montana, Shoshone and Bridger-Teton in Wyoming, and Targhee in Idaho.*

Q. Of the five national forests that border Yellowstone, this one is the largest national forest outside Alaska. Name it.

A. *Bridger-Teton National Forest, at 3.4 million acres, is larger than Connecticut.*

Q. Of the five national forests that border Yellowstone, this is the oldest in the nation, established in 1891. Name it.

A. *Shoshone.*

Q. The Grand Canyon of the Yellowstone is 20 miles long, 1,500 to 4,000 feet wide, and up to 1,500 feet deep. If you hike all the way to the bottom of the canyon and all the way back up again, would that depth be greater than, lesser than, or equal to taking the stairs to the top of the Sears Tower in Chicago (the tallest building in North America) and back down again?

A. *Equal to. The hike has been described as "five miles in and 35 miles out."*

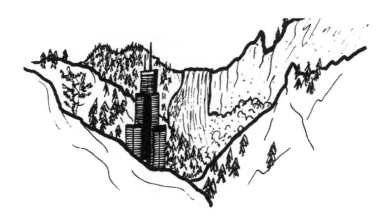

Only eleven species of tree live in the park, and eight of those are conifers.

Q. There are about 1,100 species of native plants living in the park. How many species of non-native plant live in the park?

A) 60   B) 170   C) 320

A. *B) 170, including such noxious weeds as Dalmation toad-flax, leafy spurge, ox-eye daisy, houndstongue, dande-lion, and Canada thistle.*

Q. One of the most pernicious invasive plants in the park is spotted knapweed. A typical knapweed plant can produce how many seeds each year?

A. *Up to 18,000 seeds annually, and the seeds remain viable for seven to ten years.*

Q. How many lodgepole pine seeds does it take to weigh a pound? [The seeds, not the cones.]

A) 10,000   B) 100,000   C) 1,000,000

A. *B) 100,000.*

Q. Eighty percent of the park is forested and eighty percent of the forests are lodgepole pine. Why is lodgepole so prevalent here?

A. *Because lodgepoles can tolerate the nutritionally poor, well-drained soils and the low precipitation, and they are adapted to reproduce after forest fires. Only a few kinds of trees grow here.*

Lodgepole pine cones more than 50 years old still have seeds capable of sprouting.

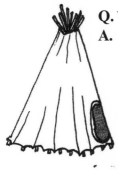

Q. Why are lodgepoles called lodgpoles?

A. *Because they are ramrod straight making them great for teepees and other Indian dwellings. The diameter of any individual tree generally does not vary much more than a single inch for every thirty feet of length.*

Q. This tree is the most widely distributed native tree in North America and is found in Yellowstone. Name it.

A. *Aspen.*

Q. True or false: Forest fires hinder the spread of new aspen trees.

A. *False: forest fires encourage the growth of new aspen trees. After a fire, researchers found that new aspen shoots were ten times more plentiful in a burned area than in an adjacent unburned area. Because the fire had cleared out other species such as sagebrush, fir, and pine, there was less competition for the abundant new nutrients left behind by the ashes. Although many animals feasted on new aspen shoots, the shoots that weren't eaten stood a far better chance of growing into adult trees.*

Q. What has happened to the number of aspen groves in Yellowstone since the park was established?

   A) 50 PERCENT INCREASE
   B) 50 PERCENT DECREASE
   C) REMAINED THE SAME

A. *B) A 50 percent decline. About half of Yellowstone's aspen groves have disappeared due to a variety of factors such as grazing by elk, fire suppression, and drought.*

Aspen is a minor species in Yellowstone covering only about 2% of the park.

Q. True or false: Aspen grow best from seeds.

A. *False: Aspen trees grow best from existing roots. Every time a beaver cuts an aspen sapling or a forest fire kills an aspen tree, new shoots spring from the root stock. Remove the beaver or remove the forest fire and there will be little new growth.*

Q. The presence of wolves in the park increases the presence of aspen. How?

A. *Wolves keep the elk moving from place to place instead of staying in a single location. This prevents elk from grazing too heavily in an area with new aspen shoots.*

> There are two types of yellow monkey flower in the park. The regular kind blooms in the summer, is about a foot high, and lines the edges of streams and springs. The other kind grows in the winter and grows to only a few inches tall. It can be found exclusively around hot springs, where the low height helps it avoid the paralyzing winter temperatures that sweep the area inches above the surface of the hot water. It is pollinated by insects that are also active in thermal areas in winter.

Q. E. B. White, author of *Charlotte's Web* and other books, wrote that the one virtue of this particular town is that you learned to spell "moccasin" when you drove through it. What Yellowstone gateway community was he referring to?

A. *West Yellowstone.*

Q. There are about 2,000 campsites in the park accessible to vehicles. How many backcountry campsites are there?

    A) 2,000   B) 1,000   C) 300

A. *C) 300.*

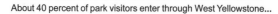
About 40 percent of park visitors enter through West Yellowstone...

Q. If you drive every road in Yellowstone, how much of the park will you have seen?

A) 2 PERCENT   B) 20 PERCENT   C) 65 PERCENT

A. *A) Two percent.*

Q. Are there more miles of hiking trails or roads in the park?

A. *Trails. There are 310 miles of paved roads and 156 miles of unpaved roads, but about 1,100 miles of backcountry trails.*

Q. What is the only section of road that remains open year-round in Yellowstone?

A. *From the north entrance at Mammoth to the northeast entrance at Cooke City, where it dead-ends in the winter.*

Q. When are roads in the park closed to wheeled vehicles for the winter?

A. *The first Sunday of November.*

Q. How much snowfall does the park receive in a typical year?

A. *Between 50 and 200 inches.*

Q. When do the roads generally open in the spring?

A. *Some of the roads are plowed open by late April; usually most of the roads are open by mid-May.*

> **The National Park Service pledges to open the south and east gates on exactly the same date every year so that neither of the tourist towns of Jackson Hole or Cody has an advantage over the other.**

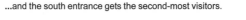

...and the south entrance gets the second-most visitors.

Q. Name the only lodges in the park that remain open year-round.

A. *Mammoth Hot Springs Hotel and Old Faithful Snow Lodge.*

Q. In an average summer, how many items are turned into the park headquarters' lost and found department?

    A) 500   B) 1,500   C) 4,000

A. *C) 4,000. Generally, items of usable clothing were donated to shelters; gear such as binoculars and cameras was donated for the use of NPS employees; and other useful items were auctioned by the General Services Administration. Recently, however, the GSA has proposed a new rule stating that all items must be destroyed.*

> The forests in Yellowstone have never been logged for timber. The valleys have never been subdivided. The rivers have never been dammed. The minerals have never been mined. The grasslands have never been grazed by livestock. Roads have not been bulldozed up every valley. Very few places in America can make these claims.

Temperature decreases about 5° F. for every thousand feet gain in elevation.

Geography Crossword

Across

2. This is the coldest month in Yellowstone
4. Something Shoshone Lake has none of
5. A very bad weed
8. The only place where boating is allowed on a river
9. This shrub can live 200 years
12. How many U.S. national parks are bigger than Yellowstone?
15. This tree is on the decline in Yellowstone
16. This peak has the highest elevation in the park

Solution on page 109

Down

1. The oldest national forest in the nation
3. 75% of the park's water ends up in this ocean
6. There are about 340 of these in the park, most of which were recently discovered
7. The tallest waterfall in the park
8. 80% of the park's forests are this kind of tree
10. Trees will not grow in this valley
11. This creek has the lowest elevation in the park
13. The percent of the park that is water
14. This lake drains to two oceans

To climb a thousand feet in elevation is equal to moving northward 300 miles.

Quote Quest ™

Find the underlined words from this quote by Ferdinand Hayden, expressing his opinion of Yellowstone Lake: "So far as <u>beauty</u> of <u>scenery</u> is <u>con-cerned</u>, it is <u>probable</u> <u>that</u> <u>this</u> <u>lake</u> is not <u>surpassed</u> by any <u>other</u> on the <u>globe</u>." *When all the underlined words have been crossed out, the remaining letters will spell out what Rudyard Kipling had to say after he looked down the throat of Riverside Geyser.*

```
T  H  I  S  N  T  D  E  S
V  E  R  L  A  O  E  O  U
O  K  A  H  Y  G  N  T  R
I  F  T  Y  R  T  R  H  P
L  G  E  T  E  G  E  E  A
Y  A  S  U  N  L  C  R  S
E  R  K  A  E  O  N  I  S
N  T  H  E  C  B  O  E  E
M  O  U  B  S  E  C  T  D
E  L  B  A  B  O  R  P  H
```

Hidden Message:

" _ _ _ _ _ _ _ _ _ _ _ _

_ _ _ _ _ _ _ _ _ _ _ "

_ _ _ _ _ _ _ _ _ _

Answer on page 107

Hike the boundary of the park and you'll cover 300 miles.

GEOLOGY

Q. The crust of cold solid rock on top of the earth is about 20 miles thick over the average continent, twice that thick under mountain ranges, and only about five miles thick under the oceans. Magma is usually found about 40 miles deep. But in Yellowstone, approximately how far under the surface of the earth does a magma chamber lie?

A) 2 MILES   B) 6 MILES   C) 11 MILES

A. *A) About two miles under Yellowstone, a bulge of magma is restlessly pressing upwards. Normally, the temperature of the earth increases 54°F. for every half mile closer to the center of the earth you get. But here, only a thousand feet down—a little more than the length of three football fields—rocks are already so hot they can heat water to an incredible 500°F.*

Q. True or false: The land in central Yellowstone has been rising at approximately the same rate as fingernails grow.

A. *True: Pushed upwards by a churning sea of magma, land in Yellowstone has been rising at the rate of around an inch per year. Occasionally it falls at the same rate.*

Q. What percent of rock in the park is volcanic?

A) 27 PERCENT   B) 59 PERCENT   C) 86 PERCENT

A. *C) 86 percent of the rock in the park is volcanic; the rest is sedimentary.*

The word caldera [call-DARE-a] comes from the Latin word that gives us "caldron."

Q. How long has it been since lava flowed from volcanic vents in Yellowstone?

A) 10,000 YEARS   B) 70,000 YEARS   C) 350,000 YEARS

A. *B) 70,000 years, forming Pitchstone Plateau in the southern part of the park.*

Q. The Yellowstone caldera is the largest known center of active volcanism on the planet. The caldera measures 45 miles by 30 miles. That's an area big enough to fit:

A) ELLIS ISLAND   B) TOKYO   C) RHODE ISLAND

A. *B) The entire city of Tokyo could fit inside the caldera.*

Q. What are the caldera's boundaries today?

A. *The rim of the caldera is visible on the drive from Madison Junction to Norris, and as the road travels from Ashton, Idaho, through Island Park and on to West Yellowstone. To the untrained eye, it simply looks like a cliff. In the years since the volcano last exploded, the caldera has been eroded, glaciated, filled with lava and ash, and covered with vegetation.*

> **Yellowstone is one of about 30 hotspots on the planet. At other places on the planet, as continental plates drift over the top of hotspots, they form chains of islands such as the Galapagos Islands, the Azores, the Aleutians, and the Hawaiian Islands. The Yellowstone hotspot is the only hotspot that's located in the middle of a continent, possibly because there was a natural weakness in the crust here or possibly because a huge ancient meteorite punched a hole through the crust like a pipeline.**

The eruption of the hotspot 2 million years ago left a hole larger than Rhode Island.

Q. The North American continental plate has been slowly sliding over the top of the Yellowstone hotspot, like a rug sliding over a rock, at a steady, sustained rate. How fast is the continental plate moving over the hotspot?

A) ONE INCH PER YEAR
B) ONE INCH PER DECADE
C) ONE INCH PER CENTURY

A. *A) About one inch per year. Around 16.5 million years ago, the hotspot was under what is now known as Nevada, near the border with Oregon and Idaho. As the continent continued to drift southwest, the hotspot moved beneath Oregon's southeast corner, then across Idaho, then into Wyoming. It's now on its way into Montana at the rate of an inch per year.*

Q. At its current rate of continental drift, how many years until the Canadian border slides over the hotspot?

A) 2 MILLION   B) 12 MILLION   C) 21 MILLION

A. *C) In about 21 million years the Canadian border will be over the Yellowstone hotspot.*

Q. During the eruption of Mount St. Helens, the total volume of ejected ash was about one-quarter of a cubic mile: equal to a giant cube of rock six-tenths of a mile on each side. During an eruption of the Yellowstone caldera two million years ago, 600 cubic miles of ash were ejected, enough to fill a cube 8.4 miles on each side. If that much material were spread evenly over the state of Montana, how deep would it be?

A) 2 FEET
B) 10 FEET
C) 20 FEET

A. *C) That's enough ash to bury Montana to a depth of 20 feet.*

The petrified tree near Tower Junction was a redwood tree.

Q. Another major blast of the Yellowstone super volcano 1.3 million years ago threw out 67 cubic miles of rock and ash, and a third eruption 630,000 years ago threw out 240 cubic miles of debris. If you combined all of the material ejected in all three of these eruptions and formed it into a solid block of rock one mile high and one mile wide, how many miles long would it be?

A) 100 MILES   B) 500 MILES   C) 900 MILES

A. *C) It would stretch 900 miles, which is equal to the distance from New York City to Atlanta, Georgia.*

Q. An eruption of the Yellowstone super volcano some 12 million years ago dumped one to two feet of ash in current-day Nebraska, suffocating numerous animals gathered around a watering hole. The remains of camels, rhinos, horses, giant tortoises, sabertooth deer, and other animals killed—and preserved—by ash can be found at Ashfall Fossil Beds State Historical Park near Orchard, Nebraska. How far from Yellowstone is this spot in Nebraska?

A. *800 miles from Yellowstone.*

Q. Approximately how many times has the hotspot erupted as the continent slowly moved over the top of it?

A) 3 TIMES   B) 50 TIMES   C) 100 TIMES

A. *C) Rocks along the path of the hotspot show about a hundred different distinct ages, indicating the hotspot has erupted a hundred different times as the continent drifted over it.*

Craters of the Moon in Idaho was formed by the Yellowstone hotspot.

Q. There are about 40 square miles of petrified forest in and around the park, forming the largest collection of standing stone trees in the world. According to one study of Specimen Ridge, how many forests have grown up and been buried under successive layers of ash at this location?

A) 4 B) 13 C) 27

A. *C) 27 different forests dating back more than 50 million years.*

Q. Yellowstone's fossil forests contain the petrified remnants of about 200 different species of plants. Scientists have found evidence of many sub-tropical species, such as mangrove, breadfruit, and magnolia, mixed in with cool climate species such as spruce, willow, and elm, and moderate-climate species such as walnut, oak, and hickory. How did so many kinds of trees live in such close proximity?

A. *Researchers theorize that tropical trees grew in the warm valleys, while temperate trees grew mid-slope, and cool-weather trees grew towards the tops of mountains. During a cataclysmic eruption, all trees were swept into the valleys where they became petrified in a tousled jumble of species. Still, at the time of the eruption, the valley floor must have been less than a thousand feet above sea level to allow such tropical trees to flourish. Some of the petrified trees were more than 500 years old when they were killed.*

> **Early explorer Jim Bridger said of the petrified forest that there were "Peetrified birds sittin' on peetrified trees singin' peetrified songs in the peetrified air."**

Q. The Obsidian Cliff in Yellowstone is one of the biggest deposits of obsidian in North America. How long is Obsidian Cliff?

A) 0.25 MILE B) 1.75 MILES C) 2.5 MILES

A. *C) 2.5 miles.*

Idaho potatoes grow well in ashes left behind by Yellowstone eruptions.

Q. Lava forms obsidian, granite, or rhyolite. What causes the different types of rock to form from the same type of lava?

A. *To form obsidian, you need a lava flow that is very thick, containing a very high level of silica and a very low level of water. Then, that wall of lava must have a head-on collision with something that cools it down extremely fast, like a large body of water or a glacial ice sheet. The lava cools so quickly it does not have time to crystallize, so it forms glass rather than rock. The same lava, when trapped underground, cools very slowly so it has time to crystallize before hardening, forming granite. If the lava cools at a moderate rate above ground, rhyolite forms. The cliff walls of the Grand Canyon of the Yellowstone are formed of rhyolite; nearby Granite Peak, the tallest mountain in Montana, is made of granite.*

Q. Native Americans used obsidian to make arrowheads, knives, and mirrors. Archaeologists have found Yellowstone obsidian as far away as Ohio, Illinois, and Mississippi. How can scientists tell that the obsidian came from Yellowstone?

A. *Every flow of obsidian has individual characteristics that can be recognized like a fingerprint.*

Q. In Yellowstone, obsidian is black. Is obsidian always black?

A. *No. Obsidian is colored according to the impurities. It's usually black but can be brown, gray, red, blue, green, orange, yellow, clear, and speckled.*

> **Obsidian is named after a man named Obsius who discovered and described the mineral in Ethiopia about 2,000 years ago. His work was mentioned by Pliny the Elder.**

Iron and magnesium typically give obsidian a dark green to brown color.

Q. Which is sharper: a knife made of obsidian or a knife made of steel?

A. *A blade made of obsidian can be honed to an edge five times sharper than high-quality surgical steel. It is sometimes used in scalpels because it produces a cleaner cut and less tissue trauma than steel blades.*

Q. Bunsen Peak at the northern edge of the park was named after:
  A) PERRY BUNSEN, AN EARLY CARTOGRAPHER
  B) SUZANNE BUNSEN, WHO RAN A STAGE STOP NEAR HERE
  C) ROBERT BUNSEN, FOR WHOM THE BUNSEN BURNER IS NAMED

A. *C) Bunsen Peak was named after Robert Bunsen, the German chemist who improved the design of the Bunsen burner, which was then named after him. Bunsen was one of the first to propose theories on what made geysers erupt. Bunsen, after studying geysers in Iceland, created artificial geysers out of test tubes in his lab in order to prove his theories correct.*

Q. Bunsen Peak is actually a:
  A) PLUG OF AN ANCIENT VOLCANO
  B) PILE OF GLACIAL DEBRIS
  C) HUGE MOUND OF TRAVERTINE

A. *A) Bunsen Peak started out as the plug of magma in the neck of a volcano that solidified and acted like a stopper. Over the eons, the volcano eroded away, leaving the plug standing alone.*

Q. 90 percent of Yellowstone was buried under ice during the last Ice Age, which ended about 10,000 years ago. How many years did that Ice Age last?
  A) 2,000   B) 17,000   C) 2 MILLION

A. *B) 17,000 years.*

Obsidian scalpels are often used in cardiac surgery and eye surgery.

Q. Marks on the rocks on the very top of the Washburn Range indicate that glaciers were once thick enough to completely cover the range. It's estimated that the ice averaged 3,500 feet deep. How many Statues of Liberty would you have to stack on top of each other to equal that depth?

A. *It would take 12 Statues of Liberty stacked on top of each other to exceed the depth of the ice, although the torch on the top statue would be poking out above the ice.*

Q. About 15,000 years ago a glacier carried Glacial Boulder from the Beartooth Mountains north of Yellowstone and deposited it near  Inspiration Point on the north rim of the Grand Canyon of the Yellowstone. The rock is 24 feet wide and 18 feet long and weighs about one million pounds. How far did it travel from its probable point of origin?

A) 1 MILE   B) 40 MILES   C) 162 MILES

A. *B) 40 miles.*

> **"Stay on this good fire-mountain and spend the night among the stars. Watch their glorious bloom until the dawn, and get one more baptism of light. Then, with fresh heart, go down to your work, and whatever your fate, under whatever ignorance or knowledge you may afterward chance to suffer, you will remember these fine, wild views, and look back with joy to your wanderings in the blessed old Yellowstone Wonderland."**
> *-John Muir, 1898*

Obsidian is slightly harder than window glass.

Geology Acrostic

Y _ _ _

The continent moves over the hot spot one inch in this time period.

E _ _ _ _

Yellowstone does this about once every 650,000 years.

L _ _ _

The rock called rhyolite is formed from this raw material.

L _ _ _

There are about 200 of these in Yellowstone.

O _ _

One of the many species of petrified trees found in the park.

W _ _ _ _ _ _ _

This mountain range has scrapes from glaciers across the top.

S _ _ _ _ _ _ _ _ _ _ _ _

About 27 different forests have grown up and been buried by ash here.

T _ _ _ _

This city could comfortably fit inside the Yellowstone caldera.

O _ _ _ _ _ _ _

This forms when lava meets water or ice, cooling quickly.

N _ _ _ _ _ _ _

In this state 800 miles from Yellowstone, ash from an explosion 12 million years ago killed many ancient animals.

E _ _ _ _

What happened to the rest of the mountain that used to be where Bunsen Peak is.

Answers on page 107

The pronghorn antelope is actually not a true antelope but is related to the goat.

Yellowstone Word Scramble

Animals

preettrum snaw   _ _ _ _ _ _ _ _ _   _ _ _ _

soyper   _ _ _ _ _ _

grouca   _ _ _ _ _ _

swelov   _ _ _ _ _ _

totatchur totru   _ _ _ _ _ _ _ _ _   _ _ _ _ _

zizgyrl   _ _ _ _ _ _ _

peenolta   _ _ _ _ _ _ _ _

ghobirn peesh   _ _ _ _ _ _ _   _ _ _ _ _

somoe   _ _ _ _ _

nobsi   _ _ _ _ _

teyoco   _ _ _ _ _ _

Things

sandiboi   _ _ _ _ _ _ _ _

tanerig   _ _ _ _ _ _ _

holteriy   _ _ _ _ _ _ _ _

tepidfier storef   _ _ _ _ _ _ _ _ _   _ _ _ _ _ _

slamufroe   _ _ _ _ _ _ _ _ _

treesyegi   _ _ _ _ _ _ _ _ _

tretrevain   _ _ _ _ _ _ _ _ _ _

gooplleed nipe   _ _ _ _ _ _ _ _ _   _ _ _ _

Places

thammom   _ _ _ _ _ _ _

sorrin   _ _ _ _ _ _

dol tafflihu   _ _ _   _ _ _ _ _ _ _

Answers on page 107

Sometimes boardwalks at Norris have to be closed when new hot springs become active.

GEYSERS & HOT SPRINGS

Q. There are an estimated 10,000 thermal features in the park including hot pools, fumaroles, mud pots, and seeps. What percent of Yellowstone's thermal features are geysers, defined as hot water that spurts forcefully out of the ground?

    A) 3 PERCENT   B) 22 PERCENT   C) 47 PERCENT

A. *A) Only about three percent, about 300 geysers.*

Q. Upper Geyser Basin (home of Old Faithful) contains the densest concentration of geysers in the world. What percent of the world's geysers are located in this two square mile area?

    A) 10 PERCENT   B) 25 PERCENT   C) 40 PERCENT

A. *B) 25 percent. Upper Geyser Basin has about 140 geysers in a single square mile.*

Q. The Firehole River where it begins above Upper Geyser Basin is a cold mountain stream with a typical mid-July water temperature of about 50°F. By the time it reaches Firehole Falls below Lower Geyser Basin—a distance of about 12 miles, as the crow flies—what is the river's water temperature?

    A) 60°F.   B) 85°F.   C) 110°F.

A. *C) 110°F. The river picks up heat as it passes through Upper, Midway, and Lower Geyser Basins. It's been estimated that the heat that goes into the Firehole River could melt seven tons of ice per minute. The output of the twin features of Excelsior Geyser Crater and Grand Prismatic Spring in the Midway Basin increases the temperature of the entire river by nearly 40°F.*

The park has only six geysers that erupt 100 feet or higher on a regular daily basis.

> **Mountain man Jim Bridger reported that the Firehole River flowed so fast that the friction of the water against the riverbed heated up the water.**

Q. Grand Prismatic Spring pumps out over 4,000 gallons of boiling water every single minute, making it the largest hot spring in:
A) YELLOWSTONE   B) NORTH AMERICA   C) THE WORLD

A. *B) North America. It's the third largest hot spring in the world. Two hot springs in New Zealand have more volume.*

Q. Grand Prismatic Spring produces nearly six million gallons of water per day, enough to fill more than 200 railroad tank cars or more than 300,000 automobile gas tanks. It's also the deepest spring in the park, at 111 feet. Is that greater than, lesser than, or equal to the average eruption height of Old Faithful?

A. *A little less than. Old Faithful varies in the height of eruptions, but the average height is around 130 feet.*

Q. Bathwater is usually around 110°F. What is the hottest temperature in which fish can survive?
A) 68°F.   B) 81°F.   C) 104°F.

A. *C) Certain specialized fish can survive 104°F. In parts of Yellowstone fish have adapted to live in water much hotter than what they normally prefer. Trout usually like temperatures between 50 to 65°F. They grow fastest at 64°F. and*  *generally cease growing at 72°F. Normally, temperatures above 77°F. will be lethal within a few hours. But in Yellowstone, trout have adapted to higher temperatures. In the Firehole River, trout thrive in temperatures up to 78°F.*

The Icelandic word "geysir" means gushing....

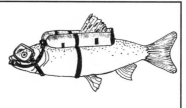

The hot water of Yellowstone has very little oxygen dissolved in it which prohibits normal fish life in many areas.

Q. Yellowstone has about 300 active geysers, more than anywhere else in the world. Outside of Yellowstone, where are the densest concentrations of geysers?

A. *Kamchatka Peninsula in Siberia, Russia (200 active geysers); Chile (80); New Zealand (51); New Guinea (38) and Iceland (25). Iceland used to have the third most geysers, but tapping them for geothermal energy destroyed many.*

Q. One geyser field in New Zealand originally had 130 geysers, but the hot water was tapped for geothermal development. How many of those geysers still erupt?

   A) 108   B) 72   C) 14

A. *C) Only 14.*

Q. There are only eleven major geyser fields on earth. How many have been left pristine, untouched, and undeveloped?

   A) THREE   B) SIX   C) TEN

A. *A) Only three: Yellowstone, Kamchatka, and Chile. The rest have been mined for their geothermal energy.*

Q. Pure water boils at 212°F. at sea level, but the boiling point drops as the elevation rises. (That's why many cooking mixes include high-altitude directions, which require the item to be cooked longer due to the lower temperatures.) In Yellowstone, the average elevation is about 8,000 feet above sea level. At this elevation, at what temperature will water boil?

   A) 206°F.   B) 199°F.   C) 189°F.

A. *B) 199°F.*

...and that comes from the Icelandic verb 'gjosa' meaning 'to gush'.

Q. At Norris Geyser Basin, magma is nearer to the surface than any other place in the park. When you drill a hole in the crust of the earth, the temperature increases the farther down you go. Normally, this temperature increase is fairly constant: 1.4°F. for every 100 feet down. However, a hole drilled in Norris Geyser Basin showed that the temperature increased much faster. How much faster?

A) 11 TIMES   B) 57 TIMES   C) 89 TIMES

A. *C) 89 times faster, at the rate of 124°F. for every 100 feet down. Therefore, water that trickles down heats up rapidly as it descends.*

Q. Super-heated water that is under a lot of pressure is unable to boil. How hot is the water 1,000 feet below the surface of Norris Geyser Basin?

A) 239°F.   B) 317°F.   C) 459°F.

A. *C) 459°F. By contrast, deep groundwater at Mammoth is only 167°F., which is not even boiling. All the bubbles coming up from springs in the Mammoth area are from carbon dioxide rather than heat. Mammoth has many hot springs but there are no geysers. This indicates that magma is much closer to the surface at Norris than at Mammoth.*

Q. In 1929 researchers drilled a test hole in Norris Geyser Basin to gather information about the rock formations and sub-surface temperatures. The drilling had to be halted once it reached a depth of 265 feet because the steam pressure in the ground was so high that it nearly blew up the drilling rig. At that depth—less than the length of a football field—what was the temperature of the water?

A) 257°F.   B) 401°F.   C) 574°F.

A. *B) 401°F. After the drill was abandoned, it was plugged with concrete, but super heated water made its way into the hole anyway, forming an entirely new geyser where none existed before. It's called the Carnegie Drill Hole Geyser.*

During the summer months, 25,000 people visit Old Faithful daily.

Joke

It's said that birds in Yellowstone drink so much hot water that they lay hard-boiled eggs.

Q. What percent of Yellowstone's thermal features are located in the backcountry far from the beaten path?

A. *Only about 25 percent. Shoshone Geyser Basin and Heart Lake Geyser Basin are the only major collections of thermal features accessible only by trail.*

Q. Yellowstone Lake has an underwater geyser which can be seen from the shore of West Thumb. Once every 25 minutes, the water roils when this submerged geyser erupts about 20 feet below the surface. Researchers sent an underwater video camera to see what was happening. They found that cutthroat trout regularly patrol the area, feeding on clouds of crustaceans and aquatic insects stirred up by the eruptions. What did they name this odd feature?

A) WHIRLPOOL WONDERLAND

B) FISH CAFÉ

C) TROUT JACUZZI

A. *C) The Trout Jacuzzi.*

Q. What percent of the more than 3 million visitors to Yellowstone annually will see Old Faithful erupt before they leave the park?

A) 50 PERCENT   B) 85 PERCENT   C) 99 PERCENT

A. *B) 85 percent. The 15 percent who do not probably skip it because they've already seen it.*

Joke

Locals boast that when the geysers freeze solid in the winter, they cut the ice into blocks and use them as foot warmers.

Water erupting at Old Faithful is 244°F.

Q. Old Faithful is not Yellowstone's tallest geyser, not the hottest, and it does not discharge the most water. It is not the most regular (Bead Geyser and Riverside Geyser are) but it does erupt on a predictable basis 20 to 23 times every day, year in, year out. What is the time span between the shortest recorded interval between eruptions, and the longest?
A) SIX MINUTES   B) 30 MINUTES   C) 110 MINUTES

A. *C) 110 minutes. The shortest recorded interval was 33 minutes; the longest interval was 148 minutes.*

Q. After timing more than 46,000 eruptions of Old Faithful, rangers found that the average eruption time was 64.91 minutes. In the years since this study, the interval has increased and is now closer to every 74 minutes. Is there a way to guess when the next eruption will be?

A. *Yes. The timing of Old Faithful is tied to the duration of the last eruption. If it was a short eruption (one to two minutes), Old Faithful will erupt again in a short time (45 to 50 minutes). If it was a long eruption (5 minutes or more), it will be a longer time before the next eruption (90 minutes or so).*

Q. What is the difference between geyserite and travertine?

A. *Geyserite or sinter, caused when superheated pressurized water dissolves silica rock such as quartz or sand and then drops it as soon as the water cools, collects around geysers at the very slow rate of about an inch every century. But travertine, caused when hot pressurized water dissolves the calcium carbonate of limestone or chalk, collects very quickly, so that the accumulation can be noticed from week to week.*

Q. Old Faithful spews about 8,500 gallons of water every eruption. That's enough water in each eruption to supply a typical American with water for how many days?
A) 10 DAYS   B) 85 DAYS   C) 212 DAYS

A. *B) 85 days, at the average rate of 100 gallons per day.*

Water in Hot Springs Basin is so acidic it dissolves the pants off people who sit on wet ground.

Q. How many pounds of dissolved silica come out of Old Faithful with each and every eruption?

A) 10 POUNDS   B) 40 POUNDS   C) 65 POUNDS

A. *C) 65 pounds. It's been estimated that about 390 tons of mineral matter from all geyser basins in the park are carried away, dissolved in water, every single day. That's about equal to the weight of a Boeing 747 jet plane.*

Q. Judging from the known rate of the average annual deposit of geyserite, scientists conclude that Castle Geyser, located in Upper Geyser Basin, with a 12-foot tall cone of geyserite, has probably been erupting in that same place how long?

YNP Formed

Medieval Age

Pyramids Built

Ice Age

A) 1,000 YEARS   B) 5,000 YEARS   C) 15,000 YEARS

A. *C) About 15,000 years, erupting ever since the last Ice Age. It's the largest geyser cone in the park and probably the oldest geyser.*

Q. How much travertine is added to the Mammoth terraces daily?

A) 20 POUNDS   B) 200 POUNDS   C) 2,000 POUNDS

A. *C) 2,000 pounds, or one ton. That's equal to the weight of a typical bison. Geologists estimate that new travertine is deposited at the regular rate of about eight inches per year.*

> **Public water supplies in some areas of the park are so high in fluoride that the excess has to be removed from the water before it can be drunk. Some springs on Pitchstone Plateau are radioactive. Levels of mercury and arsenic in the Firehole River are so high that trout that live there are unfit for human consumption.**

Travertine in the Mammoth area is more than 250 feet thick.

> **Bicyclist W. O. Owen toured the park in 1883 and decided it would be neat to make a cup of tea from the boiling hot water of a geyser. He filled his teapot with geyser water, added tea leaves, let it steep a few minutes, and then filled his belly with three cupfuls of the brew. Within the hour, Owen was seized with a sickness that laid him low for many hours. So much for teatime.**

Q. Bead Geyser in the Lower Geyser Basin (named for the round and egg-shaped beads of geyserite that tourists carried away long ago) is the most regular geyser in the park. It erupts once every 26 minutes, give or take how many seconds in either direction?

    A) 14   B) 33   C) 49

A. *B) 33 seconds.*

Q. Riverside Geyser is one of the most predictable geysers in the park. How often does it erupt?

A. *Once every six hours.*

Q. This completely unpredictable geyser is the largest geyser in the world. It throws a million gallons of water up to 300 feet in the air. Name it.

A. *Steamboat Geyser in Norris Geyser Basin. No one can predict when it's going to erupt, as it works on an odd schedule ranging from four days to fifty years. It erupted numerous times in 1911, and then was dormant until the 1960s when it went off 90 times between 1961 and 1969. Then it was dormant for nine years before erupting occasionally, but in 1982 it went off 23 times. Since then, it's erupted a few times unpredictably.*

There are two types of geyser: fountain geysers erupt intensely from pools of water...

Q. When mud pots bubble, is it because the mud is boiling?

A. *No, it's actually only trapped heated gasses bubbling through the mud that make the mud appear to be boiling.*

When hot water percolates through different minerals, it causes different colors in paint pots:	The temperature of the water at thermal features can be determined by the color of the algae living in it:
Yellow .... *sulfur* Brown .... *iron oxides* Gray ...... *manganese oxides* Orange .... *arsenic* Pink .... *clay minerals*	Pink .... *180°F* Yellow .... *160°F* Orange .... *145°F* Brown .... *130°F* Green .... *120°F*

Next to Old Faithful, Morning Glory Pool may be the single thermal feature most often visited by tourists. Long ago, the hot spring was so hot that no algae were able to grow in it, and so the crystal-clear water beautifully reflected the clear blue sky. Then people began throwing things into the water, partially clogging the vent and causing the water temperature to drop. This allowed algae to grow, spoiling the reflective effect. In 1950 rangers decided to clean the crater. They lowered the water level, which induced the spring to erupt as a geyser. Items regurgitated by the spring included $86.27 in pennies; $8.10 in other change; tax tokens from nine states; and logs, bottles, tin cans, 76 hankies, towels, socks, shirts, and underwear. In all, 112 items were removed from the throat of the spring, which improved the color of the pool.

...and cone geysers which erupt from mounds, usually in steady jets.

Thud Geyser was named because of the thudding sound from underground, caused by the expansion and collapse of steam bubbles in the plumbing. Thud is located next to where the old Fountain Hotel used to be. The hotel was torn down in 1927, but while it stood, Thud was used as a garbage disposal. In 1948 Thud was cleaned out. Here's a list of items removed from the crater, which is only 15 feet long by 18 feet wide:

a frying pan
a stew kettle
a ladle
a pie tin
a china plate
a porcelain plate
a copper plate
a blue dishpan
two knives
a spoon
a fork
a butter tub
a mixing bowl
two cake molds
an oven rack
an apron
3 one-gallon crocks
a large copper lid
animal bones
7 pop bottles
4 whiskey bottles
many beer bottles
17 tin cans
a Mason jar

a Vaseline bottle
one seltzer bottle
a broom
a duster
a towel
a bath mat
16 hankies
a linen napkin
a rubber boot
a raincoat
a cotton coat
a set of men's outer clothing
a large piece of canvas
a gunny sack
a penny
two Colorado tax tokens
a 40-gallon drum
a cog wheel
two wagon braces
two wooden kegs
several barrel staves
screen wire

pieces of scrap wire
window glass
two bricks
a horseshoe
a pitchfork
a window sash
two drawer handles
a surveyor's stake
a large piece of pipe
a kerosene lamp
a cigarette pack
a 1913 guidebook
two marbles
a film box
four shotgun shells
a light bulb (burned out)
a tree
two ear tags for cattle belonging to a Rexburg, Idaho rancher
misc. paper

It is illegal to throw anything into thermal features.

Name Games

* Constant Geyser in Norris was named by some sarcastic wit because it erupts at completely irregular and unpredictable intervals, and the eruption lasts all of five seconds.

* Spiteful Geyser in Upper Geyser Basin was originally called Spriteful, but sometime in the 1870s a cartographer made a typographical error and the "r" was accidentally left out. It's been Spiteful ever since.

* In Norris Geyser Basin there are two geysers near each other. One is named Fan Geyser and the other is named Fireball Geyser. Evidently at some point in the past the signs accidentally got mixed up, so now we have a fan-shaped geyser called Fireball and a non-fan-shaped geyser called Fan.

* Frying Pan Spring near Norris Junction was originally called Devil's Frying Pan because the bubbles that rise to the surface look and sound like grease sizzling on a griddle.

* Myriad small bubbles rising from many small springs in the bottom of Rainy Lake make it appear as if rain is falling on the surface of the water, giving rise to the name.

* Economic Geyser in the Upper Geyser Basin was named because it would shoot water 30 feet high every four to six minutes, with water going up in such a straight column that not a single drop fell out of the geyser crater, instead falling into the pool to be spurted out again. One tour guide said: "First, it never wastes its own time; second, it never wastes your time; third, it never wastes a drop of water." It is now dormant.

* Sponge Geyser in Upper Geyser Basin was named because the entire eruption could be absorbed by a sponge. It's the smallest named geyser in the park. Before the 1959 earthquake, it erupted once a minute to a height of six inches; after the quake the water level fell below the level of the surface. If it's still erupting, it cannot be seen.

Mud Pool in Norris Geyser Basin was named because it is usually completely clear.

Q. One ranger set out to remove pennies from Blue Star Pool. In the first 15 minutes he worked, how many pennies did he remove?

A) 20   B) 150   C) 700

A. *C) 700 pennies. "Shucks, one penny won't make a difference," said 700 people.*

Dragon's Mouth Spring in the Mud Volcano area has the distinction of having been named and re-named more often than any other feature in the park. Here's a list of the various names it has been known by:

*Cave Spring * The Grotto * Grotto Spring * Grotto Sulphur Spring * Gothic Grotto * Devil's Grotto * Devil's Kitchen * Devil's Workshop * Devil's Den * Blowing Cavern * Arch Spring * Belching Spring * Green Gable Spring*

On February 14, 1902, the wintertime peace of Norris Geyser Basin was shattered when a huge quantity of rock, mud, water, and steam suddenly shot skyward. A brand new geyser was born, shooting 225 feet into the air as the astonished winter caretaker watched. Because the geyser was born on February 14, it was dubbed Valentine Geyser. It still erupts, but more quietly now.

Geezer Geyser in Norris Geyser Basin was named by smart-alec naturalists in 1974.

Quote

Quest™

Find the underlined words from this Gretel Ehrlich description of Yellowstone from her book "Yellowstone: Land of Fire and Ice": "Standing in the midst of hotpots, wild gorges, and whitecapped mountains, it seemed that heaven, earth, and hell were all here in this one place, bound by the vertical stitchery of rain, snow, fire, and steam." *When all the underlined words have been crossed out, remaining letters spell out how one park visitor described the park.*

```
A  P  I  T  C  T  U  R  E  O  F  W  H  O
N  D  H  W  S  E  H  E  L  L  R  A  E  N
D  I  O  L  T  S  T  A  H  T  H  O  R  G
S  N  D  A  I  N  R  R  F  I  R  E  E  O
S  O  E  C  T  I  R  S  S  I  T  U  A  R
B  T  P  I  C  A  H  O  T  P  O  T  S  G
O  G  P  T  H  T  E  W  D  E  H  I  N  E
U  N  A  R  E  N  N  A  I  T  A  U  N  S
N  I  C  E  R  U  I  E  R  L  W  M  E  Q
D  D  E  V  Y  O  U  A  V  T  D  E  E  P
O  N  T  S  I  M  E  T  S  A  M  I  R  O
N  A  I  B  E  T  W  D  E  E  E  E  N  E
H  T  H  A  E  A  I  V  D  E  N  H  A  N
D  S  W  H  R  M  E  L  L  E  C  A  L  P
```

Hidden message:

" _ _____ __ _____

___ _____ _____

__ _ _____ _____

_____ _____ ___ ____ "

Answer on page 107

156 miles of roads are groomed for over-snow use in winter.

Thermal Features by the Numbers

ALL CLUES ARE NUMERIC AND ARE FOUND IN THE PREVIOUS CHAPTER.

Across

4. Temperature Fahrenheit of water 1,000 feet below Norris Geyser Basin
6. Approximate number of tourists who visit Yellowstone annually
8. Number of gallons of water disgorged by Steamboat Geyser when it erupts
9. Depth of Grand Prismatic Spring, in feet.
11. Number of miles of roads groomed for over-snow use in winter
13. Longest recorded interval between eruptions of Old Faithful, in minutes
15. Number of geysers located in Upper Geyser Basin
16. Number of seconds between eruptions of Bead Geyser
17. Thickness of travertine in the Mammoth area
18. Gallons of water pumped out by Grand Prismatic Spring every day
19. Year that Valentine Geyser first erupted
20. Temperature at which water boils at 8,000 feet in elevation
21. Number of pennies removed from Blue Star Pool
22. Temperature of the water that comes out of Old Faithful

Down

1. Number of people who see Old Faithful erupt daily during summer.
2. Approximate number of geysers worldwide

Answer on page 109

3. Number of gallons disgorged by Old Faithful in each eruption
5. Estimated number of thermal features in the park
7. Temperature increase in Firehole River as it passes through thermal fields
8. Number of years Castle Geyser has been erupting
10. Number of items pulled out of Morning Glory Pool
11. Temperature of the water where pink algae lives
12. Temperature at which trout grow fastest
14. Number of tin cans pulled out of Thud Geyser
16. Number of active geysers in the park
17. Pounds of travertine added to Mammoth Terraces daily
19. Year that Geezer Geyser was named
22. Percent of thermal features located in the back country

"Fumarole" is from the same root word that gives us "fumes".

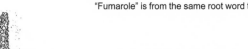

EARTHQUAKE

Q. On average, how many earthquakes will seismographs pick up in the Yellowstone area in a typical year?
A) 25   B) 100   C) 2,000

A. *C) About 2,000 small tremors. There's generally a major earthquake in Yellowstone about once every 25 years. Since 1900, the Yellowstone/Snake River region has been rocked by about 30 earthquakes of magnitude 5.5 or larger.*

Q. Name the only place in the U.S. that has more earthquakes than Yellowstone.
A) ALASKA   B) HAWAII   C) CALIFORNIA

A. *C) California.*

Q. Scientists at the U.S. Geological Survey were perplexed after the installation of a new seismograph along the southern shore of Yellowstone Lake because each winter the instrument recorded swarms of quakes that no other seismograph 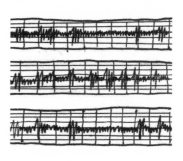 picked up. What was causing the strange quakes?

A. *The tremors were caused by the expansion and contraction of the ice covering Yellowstone Lake.*

Q. On August 17, 1959, a magnitude 7.5 quake hit the Yellowstone area at 11:37 p.m. It was centered near Hebgen Lake west of the park. True or false: This was the largest quake ever recorded in Montana.

A. *True.*

After the quake, the nearest phone that worked was 40 miles north of the park.

Q. The quake triggered a massive landslide which buried a campground and dammed the Madison River, forming Quake Lake. Half a mountain fell 1,200 feet to the valley floor below. How many seconds did it take for the landslide to hit the bottom of the valley?

A) 3 seconds   B) 8 seconds   C) 32 seconds

A. *B) Eight seconds. At that point the landslide was traveling at a speed of 174 miles per hour.*

In the Hebgen Lake earthquake, an estimated 43 million cubic yards of mountainside flew downhill, filling the valley. To put that in perspective, one million cubic yards would fill a pro football stadium. The force of this falling mass caused air and water to rush out of the area at hurricane speeds, flattening trees, hurling cars hundreds of feet, and stripping campers of their clothing. Cars were flattened to the width of a suitcase, not from being crushed by falling debris, but by the force of wind and water.

Q. How many people died in the earthquake and the resulting landslide?

A) 7   B) 28   C) 104

A. *B) 28, many of whom were sleeping at the Rock Creek Campground beside the Madison River.*

Q. How many of their bodies were never found, being so deeply buried beneath the landslide?

A) 6   B) 14   C) 19

A. *B) 19.*

Q. How long did the shaking last during that earthquake?

A. *Less than a minute.*

---

300 people were trapped between the cracked Hebgen Dam and the landslide.

Q. In the four days following the quake, how many aftershocks rattled the area?

A) 170   B) 270   C) 370

A. *C) 370.*

Q. How many geysers erupted throughout the park immediately following the quake?

A) 117   B) 179   C) 298

A. *C) 298, sixty of which had never been known to erupt before. Consider that there are only about 300 geysers in the entire park that erupt on a regular basis.*

Q. Sapphire Pool is one of the most beautifully colored hot springs in the park. Prior to the 1959 quake, it was a geyser that would erupt several times an hour with a boiling dome of water six feet high. After the earthquake, the previously clear water was roiling with mud, and eruptions blasted water 150 feet high every two hours—some of the most powerful eruptions ever seen in the park. Eventually the eruptions diminished until, by the 1970s, Sapphire was only a hot spring that occasionally overflowed. How long did it take the muddy water of Sapphire Pool to clear following the quake?

A) 12 HOURS   B) 12 DAYS   C) 12 YEARS

A. *C)12 years.*

Q. Water softener tycoon Emmitt Culligan built a home near Hebgen Lake which was designed to withstand a nuclear attack. He did not know the house straddled a fault line. How far was one end of the house lifted from the opposite end?

A: *15 feet.*

Q. What happened to Old Faithful after the quake?

A. *There was no change in the eruption pattern of Old Faithful, which erupted faithfully before, during, and after the quake.*

After the quake, a new cliff 20 feet high split Cabin Creek Campground cleanly in half.

Quote

Quest ™

Find the underlined words from this Paul Schullery quote about Old Faithful from his book "Mountain Time": "There is evidently something endearing about a natural event that has the decency to follow a human schedule." *When all the underlined words have been crossed out, the remaining letters will spell an inspiring message about geysers.*

```
L  F  O  L  L  O  W  I  F  E  Y
S  O  M  E  T  H  I  N  G  L  L
N  Y  C  N  E  C  E  D  T  E  A
A  P  S  L  I  K  E  N  G  E  A
T  E  G  E  Y  V  E  N  S  E  R
U  R  F  O  E  D  I  R  T  H  O
R  E  S  N  I  R  E  W  H  O  D
A  H  T  V  A  R  N  I  L  L  T
L  T  E  E  H  B  R  A  O  U  G
H  T  D  H  E  R  O  O  M  C  K
O  N  F  I  N  E  R  U  T  U  I
E  L  U  D  E  H  C  S  T  A  H
```

Hidden message:

"

_ _ _ _   _ _ _ _ _   _ _ _ _   _

_ _ _ _ _ _   _ _ _   _ _ _ _ _ _

_ _ _   _ _ _ _ _   _ _   _ _ _ _ _ _ _ _

"

_ _ _   _ _ _ _ _   _ _   _ _ _ _ _ _ _ _

Answer on page 108

After the quake, huge waves sloshed back and forth in Hebgen Lake for 11 hours.

FOREST FIRES

Q. In 1988, forest fires burned about 800,000 acres inside the boundaries of the park, along with 400,000 acres around the park. Is the total burned area greater than, lesser than, or equal to the size of the state of Delaware?

A. *About equal to the size of Delaware. However, only about one-third of the park burned.*

fire scars

Q. Tree ring studies dating back to the year 1525 show that minor fires swept through the area about once every 25 years, with major fires hitting about once every 250 to 400 years. Because of aggressive fire suppression efforts since the park was created in 1872, how large was the biggest fire in the park prior to 1988?

A. *The worst fire burned 20,000 acres in 1931 near Heart Lake.*

Q. Firefighters in 1931 received 30 cents per hour for their work. How much would 30 cents per hour be equal to in today's dollars?
A) MORE THAN MINIMUM WAGE
B) LESS THAN MINIMUM WAGE
C) EQUAL TO MINIMUM WAGE

A. *B) Less than minimum wage. In today's dollars, it would be worth $3.55 per hour.*

In 1931 accountants complained about the cost of the Heart Lake fire which was $87,000.

Q. The "Let Burn" policy was instigated in Yellowstone in 1972. Between 1972 and 1985, only 35,000 acres—or 1.5 percent of the land— burned. At that rate, how long would it have taken for every area of the park to burn once?

A) 100 years   B) 250 years   C) 1,000 years

A. *C) 1,000 years.*

Q. Any given plot of land in Yellowstone has burned an average of how many times since the end of the last Ice Age 10,000 years ago?

A) TEN   B) TWENTY   C) THIRTY

A. *C) Thirty times.*

Q. What percent of normal average rainfall fell in June of 1988?

A) 20 PERCENT   B) 30 PERCENT   C) 40 PERCENT

A. *A) Only 20 percent. The summer turned out to be the driest in the history of the park. The last significant rainfall of the summer happened on Memorial Day.*

Q. True or False: The summer of 1988 was the park's windiest on record.

A. *True. A total of six cold fronts blasted through the area, bringing high winds and lightning but no rain.*

Q. In an average year, how many forest fires in the park are started by lightning?

A) 4   B) 22   C) 130

A. *B) 22.*

Q. How many forest fires in the park were started by lightning in 1988?

A) 20   B) 50   C) 70

A. *B) About 50 fires.*

Deer and elk prefer to eat grasses and other green plants...

Q. Seven fires were responsible for 95 percent of the burned area in 1988. How many of these fires started outside of the park and were fought from the beginning?

A. *Five.*

Q. How many of the seven major fires were started by people?

A. *Three. (The other fires were started by lightning.) The Hellroaring Fire was probably started by an untended campfire, and the Huck Fire was caused by a tree falling across a power line. On July 22, a guy cutting firewood in Targhee National Forest just west of the park border flicked his cigarette onto the ground, starting the North Fork Fire.*

Q. The North Fork Fire was the largest single fire in Yellowstone in 1988. How many acres did this fire burn?

A. *Nearly 500,000 acres, an area about three-quarters the size of Rhode Island. It burned all the way across the park, threatening West Yellowstone, Old Faithful, and Cooke City in turn.*

Q. On July 21 park officials suspended the "Let Burn" rule and decided to fight all fires aggressively. At that time, how many acres had already burned?

    A) 17,000   B) 75,000   C) 159,000

A. *A) 17,000 acres. Some of the worst fires started after this date and were fought from the beginning.*

Q. What famous person was planning a Yellowstone vacation in the summer of 1988, but had to change vacation plans due to the fires?

A. *President George H. W. Bush. Instead, he camped out in the nearby Absaroka-Beartooth Wilderness.*

...but grasses and forbs do not grow well in mature coniferous forests.

Q. In the summer of 1988, wood lying on the forest floor contained less than two percent moisture, which is less than kiln-dried lumber. When the forest is this dry, what are the chances that an ember hitting something flammable will result in a fire?

A) 25 PERCENT   B) 50 PERCENT   C) 90 PERCENT

A. *C) At two percent fuel moisture, 90 percent of embers will start a fire.*

Q. During the fires of 1988, the park was completely closed to visitors for the first time since it opened in 1872. How long was the park closed?

A) ONE DAY   B) ONE WEEK   C) ONE MONTH

A. *A) One day: August 20.*

Q. Over the course of the 1988 summer, 25,000 firefighters saw fire duty in the park. How many news reporters covered the fires?

A. *More than 3,000 reporters showed up between July 21 and September 21. It's estimated that on any given day, 200 reporters were on duty. It was the biggest media event in the history of the National Park Service, and it was the single largest fire-fighting effort in U.S. history.*

In Jackson Hole, particulate matter in the air was 700 percent greater than normal.

Q. Of course, TV reporters and print photographers went to great lengths to show only the biggest flames they could possibly find, thereby spreading the impression that Yellowstone was an environmental Armageddon. Which large national newspaper ran an article in the summer of 1989 apologizing for their doom-and-gloom reporting of the year before, saying, "Reports of the park's death were greatly exaggerated?"

A. *The Washington Post.*

Q. Smoke plumes from the Yellowstone fires could be seen from the space shuttle. How far away did ashes fall?

A) 10 MILES
B) 20 MILES
C) 100 MILES

A. *C) Ashes fell 100 miles away in Billings, Montana, and the smoke column could be seen for 500 miles.*

Q. Some 77 helicopters and 12 fixed-wing aircraft were used in fire fighting efforts. How many cumulative hours did they spend in the air?

A) 8,900   B) 18,000   C) 39,000

A. *B) About 18,000 hours, or about 200 hours per aircraft.*

Q. Over the course of the summer, fixed-wing aircraft dropped more than seven million gallons of fire retardant, and the choppers dropped an estimated 10 million gallons of water. Ten million gallons of water is equal to:

A) THE DAILY USE IN CASPER, WYOMING (POP. 50,000)
B) THE MONTHLY USE IN CASPER
C) THE ANNUAL USE IN CASPER

A. *A) Daily use in Casper, Wyoming.*

Estimated property damage from the fires totaled more than $3 million.

Q. August 20, 1988, became known as "Black Saturday" when hurricane-force winds blasted through the park, whipping fires to a frenzy and burning 165,000 acres in one day. This was five times more acreage than had burned in the entire 116-year history of the park. Is the area burned on Black Saturday greater than, lesser than, or equal to the size of Chicago?

A. *Equal to the city limits of Chicago.*

Q. If you had been trying to outrun the fastest moving fires on Black Saturday, how fast would you have had to run?

A. *The Storm Creek fire, which was nearly out, came back to life with the high winds and traveled ten miles in three hours, or 3.3 miles per hour, about the average speed a person walks. The Hellroaring Fire advanced one mile per hour for eight consecutive hours.*

Q. What is a fire doing when it is "crowning?"

A. *When a fire burns high in the trees and spreads by leaping from treetop to treetop, rather than by spreading on the ground, it is crowning. This is also called a canopy fire. This is the fastest way fires spread, usually driven by high winds or up steep slopes. About 57 percent of the fires in the park were canopy fires; 38 percent were surface fires; the rest were grass and meadow fires.*

Q. Forest fires burn with varying degrees of heat intensity which can be likened to first-degree, second-degree, and third-degree burns. What percent of Yellowstone burned with enough heat to sterilize the soil and kill roots and seeds?

A. *Only about one percent. The rest burned moderately, meaning that seeds, bulbs, and roots beneath an inch of soil could survive and regenerate.*

Researchers weighed vegetation growing on a plot before and after a fire...

Q. When the Huck Fire and the Storm Creek Fire joined and pushed across Yellowstone, how close did the flames come to the city limits of the gateway towns of Cooke City and Silver Gate?

A) TEN MILES   B) FIVE MILES   C) ONE MILE

A. *C) One mile. A highway road sign at the entrance to Cooke City was changed to "Cooked City."*

Q. On September 7, 1988, crown fires burned to the very edge of the Old Faithful Inn compound. What crucial factor was a critical piece of luck in preventing the old wooden Inn from catching fire?

A. *The previous summer a rooftop sprinkler system had been set up to keep the wooden shingles wet in case of a fire.*

Q. On what day did snow fall, putting out the fires?

A. *Snow fell on September 11, dousing the fires. Local radio stations played Christmas carols to celebrate.*

> Although firefighting efforts employed the most sophisticated techniques and the most modern equipment available, Park Ranger Holly Bartlett summed up the situation nicely when she remarked, "A humbling quarter inch of snow accomplished what people could not."

Q. Some 67 cabins and outbuildings burned, along with 120 poles carrying electricity that burned completely and 169 poles which burned partially. How many miles of electrical lines melted?

A) 3   B) 11   C) 29

A. *B) Eleven miles.*

...The amount of vegetation 2 years after a fire was double the pre-burn volume.

Q. During a typical, normal, average fire season, it generally costs about $1,000 per acre to fight a typical, normal, average forest fire. How much was spent per acre on the Yellowstone fires?

A) $85   B) $3,000   C) $10,000

A. *A) $85. The fires were so huge that resources were spread thin and concentrated on saving structures.*

Q. $120 million was spent fighting fires over the course of the summer. That's about equal to the annual budget of:

A) HELENA, MONTANA

B) SPOKANE, WASHINGTON

C) CHICAGO, ILLINOIS

A. *B) Spokane, Washington, a city of about 200,000 people.*

Q. What percent of fire-fighting costs were for firefighter wages?

A) 26 PERCENT   B) 43 PERCENT   C) 72 PERCENT

A. *B) 43 percent went for wages; 23 percent for air support; 18 percent for supplies.*

Q. How many of the 25,000 firefighters died in the line of duty?

A) NONE   B) TWO   C) TWELVE

A. *A) Two. One was killed by a falling snag and the other in an aircraft crash.*

Q. How many tourists died in the fires of 1988?

A) NONE   B) THREE   C) TEN

A. *A) None.*

Bicknell's geranium will germinate, flower, and go to seed *only* in the year following a fire...

Q. For the large animals that died in the fires, what was the leading cause of death: burns or smoke inhalation?

A. *Smoke inhalation. Very few large animals were trapped by flames. Most large animals such as elk and bison simple moved away from the flames and continued their daily routines.*

Q. An ornithologist counted 40 ferruginous hawks flying through the heavy smoke while the fires were still burning. The birds were flying *into* the park, not away from it. These hawks are normally very rare in the park because they live on prairies. Why were they flying into the park?

A. *Prairies are a fire-prone environment, and the hawks associate the smell of smoke with a plentiful food supply, namely rodents, that are displaced by fires. Wood-boring beetles also follow the smell of smoke to feed on the dead trees, and woodpeckers follow to feast on the beetles.*

Q. Lodgepole pines produce two kinds of cones. One kind opens normally and sheds seeds regularly. But the other kind is sealed shut with resin and the seeds cannot be released unless the resin melts from the heat of a fire. As the tree ages, its branches hold more and more of these fire-activated cones, like a seed savings account. Even if the tree dies of old age or is killed by beetles, the pinecones remain viable, waiting for a fire. What temperature is required for the resin to melt, releasing the seeds?

A. *113 to 135°F.*

Q. What percent of the park is forested?
   A) 20   B) 40   C) 80

A. *C) 80 percent.*

Q. What percent of the park's forests is lodgepole pine?
   A) 20   B) 40   C) 80

A. *C) 80 percent.*

...It will never come back again until there is another fire, whether it's 5 years or 1000.

Q. One biologist found an average of 50,000 lodgepole seeds per acre following the fires. Some areas contained more than a million seeds per acre. From this amazing abundance, how many seedlings sprouted per acre on average?

    A) 100   B) 750   C) 5,000

A. *B) An average of 750 seedlings sprouted per acre.*

Q. What is the maximum average life span for a lodgepole pine?

A. *About 200 years. When lodgepoles die, they fall over and dead trees accumulate on the forest floor. Normally, dead wood on the ground is digested and broken down by fungus, insects, and bacteria. But in Yellowstone the climate is too cold and too dry to make this a speedy process. As a result, when forests go too long without fire, more and more nutrients are locked up in the deadfall and in the living trees. The forest begins slowly staving to death. A fire releases these nutrients back into the soil and begins the process over again.*

Q. Are the minerals in forest fire ashes good or bad for aquatic life in streams?

A. *Good, because the minerals act as an aquatic fertilizer. That means more plants; more plants mean more insects; more insects mean more fish.*

> **When pine needles fall into streams and lakes, the needles provide very little nutrition to aquatic plants. However, when leaves of deciduous plants and trees fall into streams and lakes, they provide much more nutrition for aquatic plants, insects, and fish. Therefore it's advantageous to the biology of streams and fisheries to have frequent fires clear the pine trees from stream banks and shorelines, leaving the land free to support grasses and deciduous species such as aspen, willow, and alder.**

Soil under an aspen grove is less acidic than under pine forests and supports more plants...

Q. How much faster will lodgepole pine seedlings in burned areas grow than seedlings in unburned areas?

A) TWICE AS FAST

B) THREE TIMES AS FAST

C) FOUR TIMES AS FAST

A. *A) Lodgepole seedlings grow twice as fast in recently burned areas because of greater sunlight reaching the forest floor and new nutrients available in the ash.*

> **Because of the greater nutrients in the plants, deer, moose and elk feeding in recently burned areas have larger antlers, higher birth rates, bigger bodies, and improved survival rates.**

Q. In the Yellowstone Ecosystem, 665 miles of hand-cut fireline and 137 miles of bulldozed fireline needed to be rehabilitated, so they were seeded with rye grass to prevent erosion. Why was rye grass chosen?

A. *Rye grass was used because it is not a perennial and will live only one or two seasons before dying out, yielding the land to native plants. Other native grasses are perennial, springing from their roots each spring.*

Q. Because of a long series of mild winters and wet summers, the elk population was at an all-time high in 1988. The park population was estimated at 30,000 to 50,000 elk. How many died in the fires?

A) 350   B) 1,250   C) 9,000

A. *A) About 350, along with an estimated 36 deer, 12 moose, 6 black bears, and possibly one grizzly.*

> **"Smokey the Bear posters which show a host of terrorized animals fleeing a wall of flames is more fiction than fact."**
>
> -George Wuerthner, *Yellowstone and the Fires of Change*

...As pines replace aspen, the animals that depend on aspen for forage diminish.

Q. About a third of the elk's grassland forage was scorched in the fires. With the rest of the rangeland already stressed from overgrazing and the drought of 1988, how many elk died of starvation during the winter that followed the fires?

A) 3,000   B) 5,000   C) 10,000

A. *B) About 5,000. However, an estimated 6,000 calves were born the next spring. Bison and deer starved too, and it's estimated that 8,000 to 12,000 large mammals died that winter. Their carcasses benefited grizzlies and eagles, both endangered species, along with innumerable other scavenger species.*

Q. How many years following a fire will a forest hit its peak level of diversity, hosting the greatest number of plant and animal species?

A) 10 YEARS   B) 25 YEARS   C) 100 YEARS

A. *B) 25 years. When a mature forest burns, there will be a 30-fold increase in the number of plant species over the next 20 years; bird species will increase up to five times. By the time lodgepole pines get large enough to shade the forest floor completely—40 to 50 years after a fire—the number of species begins to drop and it continues to drop until the forest burns again.*

> **"The resource is not twenty thousand elk, or a million lodgepole pines, or a grizzly bear. The resource is *wildness*. The interplay of all the parts of the wilderness—weather, animals, plants, earthquakes—acting upon each other to create the wild setting, creates a state of existence, a wildness that is the product and the resource for which Yellowstone is being preserved."** *-Chief Ranger Don Sholly*

Fire does not *destroy* an environment; it *rearranges* an environment.

Q. Yellowstone today supports every species of wild animal that occupied the area before the arrival of civilization. How many other places in the Lower 48 states can also make that claim?

A) NONE B) SIX C) FOURTEEN

A. *A) None.*

Match the species to its estimated population in Yellowstone:	
Cougar	25,000
Wolves	500
Grizzlies	4,000
Bighorn sheep	150
Pronghorn	700
Black bear	5,000
Moose	700
Mule deer	10,000
Bison	500
Elk	200
Employees	1,000
Summer tourists on a typical day	20

Answers next page.

Match the Number of Species in Yellowstone:	
Mammals	4
Birds	311
Fish	6
Reptiles	18
Amphibians	60

Answers next page.

Q. What percent of the 60 mammal species in the park are rodents such as voles, pocket gophers, and mice?

A) 10 B) 30 C) 50

A. *C) Almost 50 percent (27 out of 60 species) including shrews, marmots, and chipmunks.*

A beaver's teeth grow an inch per month, and wear down about as fast.

Population of Species:	Number of Species:
Cougar-------------- 20	Mammals ------------ 60
Wolves -------------150	Birds ---------------- 311
Grizzlies -----------200	Fish --------------------- 18
Bighorn sheep ----500	Reptiles ---------------- 6
Pronghorn --------500	Amphibians----------- 4
Black bear --------700	
Moose --------------700	

Rodents provide food for predators; they burrow and build tunnels which prevent the soil from becoming compacted; and they aid in plant dispersal by hiding seeds.

Population of Species:
Mule deer ------ 1,000
Bison ------------ 4,000
Elk -------------- 10,000
Employees ----- 5,000
Tourists -------- 25,000

Q. What percent of a coyote's diet is made up of rodents?

   A) 10 PERCENT   B) 33 PERCENT   C) 60 PERCENT

A. *C) 60 percent. A study done by naturalist Olaus Murie showed that pocket gophers composed 22 percent of a coyote's diet, field mice 34 percent, and rabbits, marmots, and muskrats 6 percent. Another 9 percent was grasshoppers and crickets. Coyotes also ate small amounts of grass, fish, birds, and garbage. Only one percent of a coyote's diet is deer. During winter months, carrion (mostly elk killed by wolves and winter-killed animals) becomes a major part of the coyote diet.*

> **Badgers often team up with coyotes to hunt. If the badger's digging scares the rodent and it runs out of the burrow's exit, the coyote nabs it. If it stays still hidden underground, the badger digs it up and eats it.**

A muskrat can stay underwater for 20 minutes. Their lips close behind their front teeth...

Q. This rodent, which weighs up to 90 pounds when full-grown and well fed, is the largest rodent in the park. Name it.

A. *The beaver. Second largest? Porcupine, weighing up to 45 pounds.*

Q. How much soil can a single five-ounce pocket gopher move in a typical year?

A) HALF A TON   B) ONE TON   C) FIVE TONS

A. *C) Up to five tons of soil per year. Remember that a big bison weighs about one ton.*

The lips of a pocket gopher seal behind the incisors so they don't get dirt in their mouth when digging, chewing, and biting off roots for food. To carry the roots, the gophers stuff them in their fur-lined cheek pouches which extend as far back as their shoulder blades. Then they stash their food in underground storerooms in their burrows. Bears often raid these pantries and eat the pocket gopher's entire larder.

Q. How long can a moose keep its head under water?

A) 1 MINUTE   B) 3 MINUTES   C) 20 MINUTES

A. *B) 3 minutes.*

Q. The name for this mammal comes from the Algonquin Indian term meaning, "one who eats twigs" or "one who strips bark from trees" (depending on which dictionary you look in). Name this eater of twigs and bark.

A. *The moose, which eats twigs and bark— as well as aquatic vegetation— at the rate of 40 pounds daily.*

...so they can snip, gnaw, and swallow underwater without getting water in their mouths.

Q. At one time, this mammal species inhabited the entire North American continent, having the widest distribution of any land mammal. Name it.

A. *The wolf.*

Q. At the time of Lewis and Clark, there may have been as many as 35,000 wolves in the Greater Yellowstone area. How many live in Yellowstone now?
A) 100-200   B) 500-700   C) 1,000-2,000

A. *A) The wolf population hovers between 100 and 200. There are about 300 total wolves in the Greater Yellowstone Eco-system and about 800 more in Wyoming, Idaho, and Montana combined.*

Q. How long were wolves completely absent from Yellowstone before being re-introduced in 1995?
A) TEN YEARS   B) 70 YEARS   C) 125 YEARS

A. *B) 70 years. It's thought that the last one in Yellowstone was killed in 1926.*

Q. How many wolves were captured in Canada and released in Yellowstone in 1995?
A) 11   B) 31   C) 56

A. *B) 31.*

Q. There are 100 to 200 wolves in the park, but what's the estimated population of coyotes?
A) 100   B) 500   C) 1,000

A. *C) 1,000. Coyotes were the top canine in the park until wolves were reintroduced. The impact of wolves on coyotes is mixed. Wolves sometimes kill coyotes, but coyotes feed on carcasses of elk, bison and other animals killed by wolves. Overall, however, coyote numbers have declined since the wolves returned to Yellowstone.*

The moose is the largest member of the deer family, weighing 1,000 lbs.

> Because wolves mostly cull the weak, usually the very young and the very old, they have little impact on the breeding age population of animals in the park.

Q. Which howl more: coyotes or wolves?

A. *Coyotes are the most vocal of all North American mammals. They have eleven distinct calls. After wolves returned to Yellowstone, coyotes in the area began howling more than ever before.*

Q. True or false: Wolves howl at the moon.

A. *False: wolves do not howl at the moon. Alpha wolves howl more than other wolves; bigger packs howl more than smaller packs; and lone wolves rarely howl at all. Wolves howl to keep their pack together and they howl to keep their neighbors away. They howl to attract a mate, and they howl to celebrate a successful hunt. They **never** howl while hunting.*

Q. How much meat does an adult wolf need to eat daily on average to maintain optimum health?

A. *Four pounds. They may go days without eating and then gulp down 20 pounds at a single time.*

Q. How many states outside the Greater Yellowstone area maintain populations of wolves?

A. *Five: Washington, Michigan, Wisconsin, Minnesota, and Alaska.*

> When traveling, a wolf carries its head and ears erect and alert. When hunting, the head stays low and the ears are back, forming a smooth line that blends into the background.

Moose antlers, which are shed every winter, weigh up to 90 pounds.

Q. True or false: Experts can estimate the age of an elk by the size of the antlers.

A. *False: The size of antlers is dependent upon nutrition, not age. They are shed every year, and new ones grow over the course of the summer.*

Q. It's estimated that about 10,000 elk live in Yellowstone National Park, making it the park's most numerous large mammal. By comparison, there are only about 4,000 bison, 1,000 deer, and 500 pronghorn antelope. Why are there so many more elk than any other animal?

A. *Because they have such a wide appetite. They eat the sedges and rushes in the marshes; they eat the grasses in the meadows; they eat the needles, bark, and leaves in the forest. Their adaptability makes them so versatile that they once roamed North America from coast to coast and from Canada to Mexico.*

During the spring and summer, antlers are covered in "velvet," which is a specialized type of skin that carries blood, calcium, and nutrients to the growing antlers. During the summer when an elk's rack is covered with velvet, it also acts as an air conditioning system. The blood flows through the velvet, nourishing the antlers and cooling the blood. An injury to the velvet will result in deformed antlers. When the antlers reach full growth in the fall, the velvet rubs off. Bulls that are sick, injured, underfed, or full of parasites will grow small, crooked antlers. Female elk gauge the health of a potential suitor by the size of his rack: big antlers indicate a mate who is in good health and most likely to sire healthy offspring.

There are about 3,500 wolves living in the Midwest, mostly in upper Michigan and Minnesota.

> **What good are antlers? Besides advertising the
> health of the male elk to a female, antlers serve as
> a way of testing strength against other elk. The
> antlers are perfectly designed to engage another
> set of antlers in shoving matches that determine
> which elk is stronger. The weaker elk leaves; the
> stronger elk breeds. In addition, antlers are handy
> to have for securing more food: bull elk have been
> seen thrashing trees simply to knock down veg-
> etation so they can eat it. They also use their ant-
> lers to scratch various parts of their body with
> great delicacy and precision.**

Q. Does a fully developed rack of elk antlers typically weigh:

A) LESS THAN AN AVERAGE 5-YEAR-OLD CHILD

B) MORE THAN AN AVERAGE 5-YEAR-OLD CHILD

C) THE SAME AS AN AVERAGE 5-YEAR-OLD CHILD

A. *C) A pair of antlers in a mature, well-nourished elk weigh up
to 40 pounds, which is equal to the weight of a typical American kindergartner. The male will carry them for about 140 days
before declining hormone levels cause them to drop off.*

Q. Elk have antlers. Bison have horns. What's the difference?

A. *Horns are permanent bony growths. Antlers are bony growths,
usually branched, which are shed and re-grown every year.*

Q. Nearly 100,000 elk live in the Greater Yellowstone Ecosystem. It's the largest collection of elk in North America. What
percent of the herd dies during an average winter?

A) 5 PERCENT   B) 15 PERCENT   C) 25 PERCENT

A. *B) 15 percent, mostly the old, young, and sick—and the prime
breeding bulls which spend so much time protecting their
harem that they do not have time to eat in the autumn, and
therefore go into the winter without enough fat.*

Elk antlers, one of the fastest growing animal tissues known, can grow an inch per day.

> Regular browsing by elk forces shrubs to bud from lower, less accessible branches rather than top branches. This makes for thick, brushy stands rather than tall, spindly stands.

Q. What percent of elk calves born each year are killed by predators such as bears, mountain lions, wolves, and coyotes?

A) 10 PERCENT   B) 25 PERCENT   C) 50 PERCENT

A. *B) 25 percent. Predators such as wolves and bear often make a habit of searching elk calving areas, hoping to find newborn calves lying hidden in the vegetation.*

Q. How much does a newborn elk calf weigh?

A) 10-15 POUNDS   B) 25-40 POUNDS   C) 50-65 POUNDS

A. *Elk calves weigh 25 to 40 pounds. (By comparison, a typical beagle weighs about 25 pounds.) If calves are born too small, they might not be big enough to survive when winter comes. If they are born too large, they may get stuck in the birth canal, killing the mother as well. Twins are rare. Elk calves have very little scent in order to remain practically invisible to the noses of predators.*

> When a cow elk barks, that's the signal for the calf to drop to the ground and hide. When the cow gives a high-pitched nasal whine, that's the signal to come out of hiding.

Q. The Amazon River has thousands of species of fish. Many typical American mid-western rivers have about 200 species of fish. How many species of fish live in Yellowstone?

A) 18   B) 352   C) 1,547

A. *A) 18. Twelve are native and six were introduced. By comparison, Montana has 90 species of fish, 56 of which are native.*

Horses can run faster than elk, but elk run better in brushy cover and rough terrain.

> Yellowstone is an active volcanic region at a very high elevation in a very cold environment that recently was covered by glaciers. All these factors have prohibited the spread of many fish species.

Q. Lake trout are an invasive species that often ruin native fisheries by throwing the ecology of a lake off-kilter. Some lakes where lake trout have appeared have been wiped clean of most native species. Lake trout are not native to Yellowstone. How did they end up in Yellowstone Lake?

A. *Lake trout were probably illegally released into the lake by some fishing enthusiast.*

Q. The first lake trout was caught in Yellowstone Lake in 1994; the following year, fishermen were reeling them in by the dozens. What control methods have been undertaken in a race to keep the population in check?

A. *Biologists caught a number of pregnant lake trout, fitted them with radio tracking devices, and tracked them to their spawning areas. Now every year, biologists drag gill nets over the spawning beds to try to stem the population.*

Q. The cutthroat trout, once found in great numbers all across Wyoming, Montana, Idaho, Utah, and Nevada, has been reduced to only ten percent of its original range. Lake trout now threaten the primary home of a rare subspecies known as the Yellowstone cutthroat. On average, how many cutthroat trout will an adult lake trout eat annually?

    A) 10   B) 90   C) 340

A. *B) 90. Adult lake trout mostly eat other fish, and the young eat plankton, aquatic insects, and crustaceans.*

An average porcupine has how many quills? 30,000.

Q. How many species of birds and mammals are connected, in some way, to the cutthroat trout in Yellowstone Lake?

A) 14   B) 26   C) 42

A. *C) 42, including bears, pelicans, ospreys, eagles, and otters.*

Q. If lake trout wipe out cutthroat trout in Yellowstone Lake, will it make any difference to these animals and birds?

A. *Yes, because many animals that eat cutthroat trout do not or cannot eat lake trout. For example, lake trout spawn deep in the lake rather than in shallow tributary streams like cutthroat trout, so bears generally cannot catch them. Lake trout also stay far below the surface where pelicans, eagles, and ospreys cannot reach them. Even human fishermen will be affected because lake trout are harder to catch than cutthroat trout.*

Q. On what percent of dives will an osprey successfully capture a fish?

A) 11   B) 47   C) 82

A. *B) 47 percent. In Yellowstone, about 93 percent of the osprey's diet is cutthroat trout.*

Q. What percent of the lakes and streams in Yellowstone contain no fish at all?

A) 10 PERCENT   B) 25 PERCENT   C) 40 PERCENT

A. *C) 40 percent contain no fish at all due to water temperatures that are too high, deadly acid or alkali levels from thermal features, or barriers to fish movement such as waterfalls.*

Q. In Yellowstone, the only fishing allowed is catch-and-release (except for lake trout, which fishermen are encouraged to catch-and-kill). One study found that the average cutthroat trout in Yellowstone is hooked and returned to the water how many times per season?

A) ONCE   B) TWICE   C) TEN TIMES

A. *C) Ten times.*

There are approximately 100 osprey nests in the park.

A study showed that cutthroat trout are 16 times easier to catch than brown trout, and brook trout are nine times easier to catch than brown trout. (Brown trout were introduced to the park and are not native to North America.)

Q. Fishing with a worm on a hook results in the death of about 50 percent of the fish if they are released, because many of the fish swallow the hook so deeply that they are fatally injured. This is one of the reasons why bait fishing is prohibited in the park. What percent of fish caught with fly-fishing techniques die of their injuries?

A) 2 PERCENT   B) 10 PERCENT   C) 20 PERCENT

A. *A) Two percent. Most fly-caught fish are hooked in their lips or mouth, where hooks do less harm and can be more easily removed.*

Q. Which weighs more on a typical 10- to 12-pound bald eagle: the skeleton or the feathers?

A. *The skeletal structure weighs half a pound but the 7,000 feathers weigh a pound. The bones are very light because they are hollow and filled with air.*

Q. This bird is North America's largest waterfowl, weighing about 30 pounds with a wingspan of eight feet. Name it.

A) GOLDEN EAGLE   B) OSPREY   C) TRUMPETER SWAN

A. *C) The trumpeter swan.*

Q. How many pounds of food will a trumpeter swan eat in a day?

A) 5 POUNDS   B) 10 POUNDS   C) 20 POUNDS

A. *C) 20 pounds of aquatic vegetation daily.*

Q. True or false: The neck of a trumpeter swan is equal to the length of its body.

A. *True. They do not dive underwater like loons and some ducks, but their long necks help them reach underwater vegetation.*

Harlequin ducks are the rarest breeding waterfowl in the ecosystem.

Q. Once there were hundreds of thousands of trumpeter swans in North America but they were hunted to the brink of extinction because of their beautiful feathers and tasty meat. In 1932 there were only 69 swans left in the world, and they lived at Red Rock Lakes National Wildlife Refuge near Yellowstone. How many trumpeter swans are there in North America today?

A) 2,000   B) 12,000   C) 20,000

A. *B) About 12,000. About 300 trumpeter swans live year-round at Red Rock Lakes, with another 2,000 stopping by during migration. Red Rock Lakes National Wildlife Refuge is home to the largest breeding population of trumpeter swans in the lower 48 states.*

Q. Molly Islands in Yellowstone Lake is the only place where pelicans breed in a national park. The islands total less than an acre in size. How many pelicans breed there?

A) 40   B) 250   C) 2,000

A. *C) 2,000. This is why Molly Islands are off limits to humans. If disturbed, pelicans will abandon their nests and eggs.*

> **At Mammoth the hot springs bubble not with heat but with escaping carbon dioxide. Plants love carbon dioxide, so they grow thick and lush around the edges of these pools. The plants attract birds. Birds have a very high rate of respiration, so they often succumb to the carbon dioxide which, being heavier than air, collects in low areas. The birds become unconscious and die. In one six-month period, 236 birds of 24 different species died this way at two springs at Mammoth. Coyotes and foxes often come to see if there's a free meal waiting for them at these particular spots.**

The birds on Yellowstone Lake eat an estimated 300,000 pounds of fish annually.

Q. On average, how many large mammals are killed by cars on Yellowstone roads every year?

    A) 10   B) 100   C) 1,000

A. *B) More than 100, including 14 different species, many of them rare. Excessive driving speed is the most common cause of these accidents.*

Q. True or false: The park's protection even includes bacteria and algae that live in the hot water of thermal areas.

A. *True. Delicate colonies of bacteria and algae can be destroyed when people walk, sit, swim, or soak in the hot water in which they live.*

Q. Are there more different species of mosquitoes or bees living in the park?

A. *There are 40 species of mosquitoes but 80 species of bees.*

Q. Are there more species of butterflies or moths in the park?

A. *There are 200 kinds of butterflies but 2,000 kinds of moths—and 2,000 species of beetles as well.*

> **Some insects thrive at higher than normal temperatures. In Yellowstone, ephydrid flies are often found in large numbers on microbial mats that float on the surface of hot water. About 500 adult flies can be found in a single square yard. One type of spider that eats these flies lives at the cooler edges of the mats, making occasional mad dashes onto the mats to catch the flies. The spiders can survive the heat if they move quickly. Other insects including dragonflies, beetles, and wasps also eat the flies, along with some birds such as killdeer. In winter ephydrid flies remain active but stay very close to the mats; they cannot survive in the cold air inches away from the hot springs.**

The pronghorn antelope is the fastest animal in North America.

Quote
Quest ™

Find the underlined words from this new twist on an old song: "Oh give me a home where the buffalo roam, where the deer and the antelope play; where seldom is heard a discouraging word, 'cause what can an antelope say?" *When all the underlined words have been crossed out, the remaining letters spell out another version of the same old song.*

```
O  H  G  E  P  O  L  E  T  N  A  I
D  I  S  C  O  U  R  A  G  I  N  G
V  E  W  M  W  H  E  R  E  D  E  A
B  H  Y  O  O  M  E  W  E  H  E  C
M  U  R  A  R  E  T  E  D  H  E  A
O  B  F  U  L  D  R  R  F  F  A  U
D  L  O  F  R  P  A  O  A  M  E  S
L  A  N  D  A  E  I  W  I  M  L  E
E  L  S  H  H  L  O  W  O  Y  E  O
S  U  A  W  H  R  O  H  O  U  V  S
E  W  H  I  T  O  H  A  Y  R  I  E
A  A  L  L  Y  A  M  E  S  A  G  S
T  Y  K  I  T  M  C  H  E  N  S  D
```

Hidden message:

"_ _   _ _ _ _   _ _   _   _ _ _ _

_ _ _ _   _ _ _   _ _ _ _ _

_ _ _ _   _ _ _   _   _ _   _ _ _ _

_ _ _   _   _ _ _ _ _   _ _ _ _   _

_ _ _ _ _   _ _ _ _ _   _ _ _ _ _ _ _ "

Answer on page 108

A pronghorn can cover 20 feet in a single running leap.

BEARS

Q. How many pounds of food will a grizzly eat in a typical day?

A) TEN POUNDS   B) 35 POUNDS   C) 50 POUNDS

A. *B) 35 pounds. Bears may spend 20 out of every 24 hours eating, consume 20,000 calories daily, and gain 40 pounds of weight every week. That would be like a human eating 40 hamburgers and 40 ice cream sundaes every day. Bears can weigh twice as much in the fall as they did in the spring.*

Q. One delicacy for Yellowstone bears is a small insect, the army cutworm moth. In the summer these moths congregate at high elevations, feeding on plant nectar and clustering together in large numbers in alpine rockslides. Bears roam these areas, turning over boulders, and lapping up moths. How many moths can a bear eat in a day?

A) 500-1,000   B) 5,000-10,000   C) 20,000-40,000

A. *C) Up to 40,000 moths per day.*

Q. Why do bears like to eat these moths?

A. *Per ounce, army cutworm moths are higher in calories than any food that bears eat in Yellowstone.*

Q. How can a biologist tell, by examining a grizzly bear's teeth, how old a bear is?

A) BY THE NUMBER OF TEETH. THE MORE TEETH, THE OLDER THE BEAR.

B) BY THE COLOR OF THE TEETH. THE DARKER THE TEETH, THE OLDER THE BEAR.

C) BY THE RINGS OF THE TEETH, WHICH GROW LIKE THE RINGS OF A TREE. ONE RING FOR EVERY YEAR.

A. *C) The rings of the teeth grow like the rings of a tree.*

Bears have 42 teeth.

Q. What is the hump on a grizzly's back made of?

A) FAT, TO FEED THEM DURING THE WINTERS
B) MUSCLE, TO HELP THEM DIG LIKE A STEAM SHOVEL
C) BONE, TO PROTECT THEIR SPINAL CORD DURING BEAR
  BRAWLS

A. *B) Muscle, to aid in digging. Bears dig for food and to make dens.*

Q. Which weighs more: an average, well-fed, full-grown male grizzly in Yellowstone or a Volkswagen Bug?

A. *The Volkswagen outweighs the bear: 2,000 pounds vs. 500 pounds. In coastal Alaska, where bears eat a high protein diet of salmon, bears can weigh 800 to 1,000 pounds—still less than a Volkswagen Bug.*

Q. Where did grizzly bears get their name?

A. *The word "grizzly" sounds like "grisly," which means gruesome, but it actually comes from the word "grizzled," which means streaked with gray. It is a reference to the silver-tipped hairs in the bear's fur.*

Q. How often will a female grizzly typically give birth?

A) ONCE A YEAR   B) EVERY OTHER YEAR   C) EVERY 3 YEARS

A. *C) Once every three years, to one, two, or three cubs, depending on how plentiful the food supply is.*

Q. What percent of grizzly cubs die in their first year of life?

A) 10 PERCENT   B) 25 PERCENT   C) 40 PERCENT

A. *C) About 40 percent.*

A grizzly's claws are about 4 inches long - about the length of a human finger.

Q. A male grizzly bear can roam over how much territory?
   A) AN AREA THE SIZE OF MANHATTAN ISLAND
   B) AN AREA THE SIZE OF THE CITY LIMITS OF SPOKANE, WA
   C) AN AREA THE SIZE OF RHODE ISLAND

A. *C) Rhode Island: an adult male grizzly's home ground will cover 500 to 1,000 square miles. (The entire park is 3,472 square miles!) A lot of territories overlap, but grizzlies still need lots and lots of room to roam. Female grizzlies will cover 500 square miles or less.*

Q. True or False: When bears hibernate, they go to sleep in the fall and don't wake up again until spring.

A. *False: bears sleep lightly during hibernation. Whereas the body temperature of a true hibernator such as a chipmunk falls to near freezing, sending it into a deep sleep that is difficult to awaken from, a bear's body temperature drops only 5 to 9 degrees from its normal temperature of about 100°F. Bears awaken any time their body temperatures dip below 89° in order to get their circulation going again. Furthermore, bears awaken easily when in danger, and females awaken to give birth. Bears may even emerge from their dens for short periods, and then go back inside. But when bears are sleeping in their dens, their hearts slow from 40 or 50 beats per minute to 8 to 10 beats per minute and their breathing slows as well. Their kidneys and digestive systems shut down entirely. They do not eat, drink, pee, or poop. Urine is reabsorbed. They leave their dens in March, April, or May, depending on the weather, their health, and their remaining fat.*

Q. What percent of its body weight will a bear lose during hibernation?
   A) 10-15 PERCENT   B) 20-25 PERCENT   C) 30-40 PERCENT

A. *C) A male griz will typically lose 30 percent of his body weight and a female will lose 40 percent or more if she is nursing cubs.*

The population density of grizzlies in the park is about 10 for every 1,000 square miles.

Q. Since the reintroduction of wolves in Yellowstone, have bears been waking up in the winter more often, less often, or the same amount?

A. *Bears have been waking more often in order to feed on carcasses of animals killed by wolves.*

Q. A bear cub weighs about one pound when it is born in the den in January. How much will the cub weigh when it first comes out of the den, having eaten nothing but mother's milk since birth?

A) 5 POUNDS   B) 10 POUNDS   C) 20 POUNDS

A. *C) About 20 pounds.*

Q. True or False: A griz returns to the same den every winter.

A. *False: A grizzly usually builds a new den every year and will seldom re-use a den that another bear built. A bear builds its den so the entryway captures the blowing snow, acting as camouflage and insulation. It will often be built underneath tree roots which support the walls of the den and prevent it from collapsing. The den faces north so that the entrance won't thaw out during warm spells in the winter.*

Q. What types of sounds do grizzlies make?

A. *Grizzlies snort, growl, roar, blow, and make a popping sound with their teeth. A young cub that is suckling and content will "purr" like a cat, except it's a buzzing noise that sounds more like a swarm of bees.*

Q. From a standing start, how fast can a grizzly run 100 meters?

A) 6 SECONDS   B) 20 SECONDS   C) 60 SECONDS

A. *A) Six seconds.*

Q. What's the world record for a human running a 100-meter dash?

A. *9.85 seconds, by Justin Gatlin in 2004. If a grizzly kept up its speed, it could cover 164 meters in the same amount of time.*

Cow milk is about two to four percent fat, but grizzly milk is 50 percent fat.

Q. In 2003 there were 1,746 reports of bear sightings in the park, including 1,003 grizzly bear sightings, 636 black bear sightings, and the rest unidentified. What percent of bear sightings resulted in bear-caused traffic jams?
A) 17 PERCENT   B) 27 PERCENT   C) 79 PERCENT
A. *B) 27 percent.*

Q. In what year was the first radio-collar invented?
A) 1938   B) 1954   C) 1966
A. *B) In 1954 Robert LeMunyan invented the first crude radio-collar and tried it out on a woodchuck. He was only able to track the animal as long as it didn't get more than 25 yards away. Modern science now presents a new, improved radio collar: a transmitter emits signals to orbiting satellites, pin-pointing the location of the animal for up to 253 days. When the batteries die, the scientist presses a button and two small needles mounted in the collar inject an anesthetic into the animal. The humans swoop in, replace the old batteries with fresh ones, and the animal awakens.*

Q. Between 1931 and 1941, when feeding bears at dumps and by the roadside were common events in Yellowstone, an average of 59 tourists were injured every year by bears, both black bears and grizzlies. That was one injury for every 6,336 tourists. At this rate, if adjusted for the number of visitors today, how many people would be injured by bears every year?
A. *About 475, but actually only 1.4 visitors are injured annually by bears. Injuries have been reduced because of better education of park visitors and the elimination of human food available to bears.*

Q. Of the 32 bear injuries that occurred in the park between 1980 and 2002, what percent of victims were male?
A) 34 PERCENT   B) 52 PERCENT   C) 78 PERCENT
A. *C) 78 percent.*

Female grizzlies will sometimes baby sit each other's cubs and will adopt cubs as well.

Q. In the 1920s, during the heyday of hand-feeding bears along park roads, rangers received a phone call from a distraught tourist insisting that a particular black bear must be killed because it was a menace. Arriving on the scene, rangers found that the woman had been enticing a black bear to stand up on its hind legs to reach a tasty morsel of food she held above its head, and a throng of tourists had gathered to photograph the event. The bear, after snatching a tidbit from the woman's fingers, dropped to the ground, but in doing so, its claws accidentally caught the straps of the woman's dress and stripped her naked in front of the camera-happy crowd. She had not been injured, but the woman insisted that the bear should die for causing her such humiliation. Did the rangers oblige her and shoot the bear?

A. *No, the bear was not harmed.*

Q. It has been estimated that around 100,000 grizzly bears roamed the United States in 1800. Now there are fewer than 1,000 in the Lower 48 states. How many of those live in the Greater Yellowstone Ecosystem?
A) APPROX. 50   B) AROUND 100   C) ABOUT 600

A. *C) About 500 to 600. Most of the rest live in the northern Rocky Mountain region around Montana's Glacier National Park. By comparison, about 30,000 grizzlies live in Alaska.*

Q. When grizzlies were listed as endangered in 1975, how many bears lived in the Greater Yellowstone Ecosystem?
A) 100-200
B) 200-300
C) 300-400

A. *B) About 200 to 300. In the thirty years since then, their numbers have doubled.*

98% of the original range of the grizzly in the Lower 48 is no longer occupied by grizzlies.

> During the 1959 earthquake, a bear was trapped in its den in Firehole Canyon. When a maintenance worker was attracted to the sound of the bear trying to dig its way out six days following the quake, he helped pry loose some of the larger rocks, releasing the bear— who reportedly made a beeline for the nearby river to quench a six-day thirst.

Q. True or false: A grizzly bear has the slowest rate of reproduction of any North American land mammal.

A. *False: The grizzly has the* second *slowest rate of reproduction among North American land mammals. The musk ox has the slowest rate of reproduction, with a female giving birth to a single calf once every other year.*

Q. In the Greater Yellowstone Ecosystem, which includes all the land that surrounds the park, only one percent of the property is privately owned. What percent of conflicts between bears and people occur on this one percent of privately owned property?

A) 1 PERCENT   B) 27 PERCENT   C) 66 PERCENT

A. *C) 66 percent.*

Q. In one study, 84 Yellowstone bears were tracked by their radio collars. What percentage of the bears spent at least some time outside the park boundaries?

A. *90 percent.*

Q. Before they were protected by the Endangered Species Act, what percent of grizzly bears that wandered outside the boundaries of the park ended up being shot?

A) 10 PERCENT   B) 20 PERCENT   C) 45 PERCENT

A. *C) 45 percent.*

A black bear's hearing is about twice as sensitive as a human's hearing.

Q. During a decade-long study done by the Craighead brothers in the 1960s, how many grizzlies did they find that died of old age?

A) 1   B) 39   C) 147

A. *A) The Craigheads were able to find only a single bear that died of old age. The average lifespan of a Yellowstone grizzly at that time was six years—a problem when you consider that a female griz doesn't mate until she is five or six years old.*

Q. What is the maximum life span of a grizzly?

A) 10 YEARS   B) 15 YEARS   C) 30 YEARS

A. *C) Grizzlies can live up to 30 years in the wild.*

Q. Are there more black bears or grizzly bears in Yellowstone?

A. *Black bears: about 500 to 600 black bears compared to 350 to 400 grizzlies.*

Q. How do you tell the difference between a black bear and a grizzly?

A. *Black bears have a straight face profile whereas the face profile of a grizzly is more like a dog's, with a dip from the eye to the muzzle. Black bears do not have a shoulder hump; black bears are smaller; black bears have ears that are pointier than a grizzly's rounded ears.*

Joke

How do you tell the difference between a grizzly bear and a black bear? Climb a tree. If it climbs up after you, it's a black bear. If it pushes the tree down, it's a griz.

Grizzlies never snarl. They don't have the kind of lip muscles needed.

Q. Which is the better tree climber: black bears or grizzlies?

A. *Black bears climb trees better because their claws are short and curved, like a cat's claws (except they are not retractable). Grizzlies grow claws that are so long they cannot grasp the tree as well as a black bear's claws. However, grizzlies can climb trees that have branches situated like rungs on a ladder.*

Q. How many states maintain populations of black bears?
    A) 9   B) 21   C) 32

A. *C) 32, as well as all the provinces and territories of Canada except Prince Edward Island. Black bears have lost 60 percent of their original range; they used to live in 49 out of 50 states (Hawaii was the exception).*

Q. How much does an adult male black bear weigh?

A. *300 to 500 pounds, compared to 500 to 800 pounds for an adult male grizzly.*

Q. True or false: black bears see in black and white only.

A. *False: black bears see in color.*

Q. Are black bears always black?

A. *No, black bears can be black, cinnamon, silver-blue, and can even have a white patch on their chest.*

Q. In the past century on the North American continent, have black bears or grizzly bears killed more humans?

A. *Grizzlies. Black bears have killed about 35 people in the past century and grizzlies have killed about 80 people. About 70 percent of the people killed by grizzlies got between or too close to a mother bear and her cubs.*

Black bears shed their footpads every winter like calluses falling off.

Quote Quest™

Find the underlined words from this Paul Schullery quote from his book "Mountain Time": "Being mauled by a grizzly bear has always struck me as one of those wilderness experiences where the novelty wears off almost right away." *When all the underlined words have been crossed out, the leftover letters will spell out a personality trait common to bison.*

```
T H G I R A I T I S E S
A I D T L H D A S T X Y
O U C M A E N T H Y P S
E R O D L A R B T A E S
E S U U F U F L G L R E
T R A O C A E L N W I N
O M E K F V A N I A E R
Y W H H O F E R E Y N E
E I T N W W Y B B S C D
G R I Z Z L Y A E A E L
N T S W E A R S W A S I
E S O H T T O G O A R W
```

Hidden message:

"__ __ __ __ __ __ __ __ __ __ __ __ __ __ __

__ __ __ __ __ __ __ __ __ __ __ __ __ __

__ __ __ __ __ __ __ __ __ __ __ __ __ __

__ __   __ __"

Answer on page 108

Buffalo, New York was named for the bison that once lived in the area.

BISON

Q. What's the difference between a bison and a buffalo?

A. *The difference is in skull structure, a hump, and an extra pair of ribs—14 for bison, 13 for buffalo. True buffalo live mainly in Africa and Asia; bison live in the U.S.*

The African Cape Buffalo

Q. The bison, weighing up to 2,000 pounds, is the largest land mammal in the Lower 48 states. What are its closest rivals for size?

A. *Grizzly bear and moose.*

Q. A staple of the Indian diet was pemmican, made by drying meat (especially bison meat), pounding it into a fine powder, adding melted bison fat, and packing it into rawhide bags. It was high in fat and protein; it was easily transportable; and it could be eaten without being cooked. It also kept well without spoiling. How long could pemmican last without going bad?

A) 1 YEAR   B) 5 YEARS   C) 30 YEARS.

A. *C) 30 years. Sometimes berries were added to improve the taste, but berries cut down on the length of time pemmican would keep without spoiling.*

Q. True or false: It's thought that the bison herds of the western U.S. were the greatest concentration of a single mammal species ever to exist on the earth.

A. *True. The bison's original range stretched from Alaska to Georgia.*

Joke
It's said that bison moved so fast they could eat breakfast in Texas, dinner in Oklahoma, and supper in Kansas.

Which have horns, male bison, female bison, or both? *Both.*

Q. In the 1800s, how many years did it take to reduce the bison herds, estimated at 30 to 60 million animals, to just a few thousand?

A) 10 YEARS   B) 30 YEARS   C) 60 YEARS

A. *C) Ten years. The most radical decline in bison happened between 1870 and 1880 when the railroads arrived. The railroads delivered large numbers of people with guns, and trains hauled away large numbers of hides.*

Q. The railroads shipped 1,508,000 bison hides from Montana to St. Louis in 1873. By 1882, records show 200,000 bison hides being shipped from Montana and Dakota territories. In 1883, 40,000 hides were sent back east. How many bison hides were shipped in 1884?

A. *None, by this time only a few bison remained. The great herds had been killed off.*

Q. When was the first legislation enacted to protect the bison?

A. *1894, with the National Park Protective Act which prohibited hunting in the national parks.*

Q. When Yellowstone National Park was established in 1872, about 300 to 400 bison lived within the park boundaries. Poachers picked them off one by one. By 1902, how many survived?

A. *Only 20, at which point Congress authorized the purchase of 21 bison from private ranchers around the country at a cost of $15,000. The combined herd was set up on a bison ranch in Lamar Valley and today's herd grew from it.*

Q. How many bison live in Yellowstone today?

A. *About 4,000.*

Three dairy cows are equal to one bison in grazing impact.

> When a bison ranch was in operation in the Lamar Valley of Yellowstone, rangers sometimes stampeded the bison for the sake of tourists and film crews. The stampeded bison can be seen in a key scene in the 1924 Zane Grey movie, *The Thundering Herd.*

Q. How many bison live in America today?
A. *About 350,000, compared to about 100 million cattle.*

Q. What percent of the bison in the U.S. are privately owned?
A. *90 percent.*

Q. What media mogul is also the nation's single largest bison rancher?
A. *Ted Turner, who owns about 30,000 head.*

Q. Are there any other places in the U.S. where bison roam freely as they do in Yellowstone?
A. *Yes, in Alaska several hundred bison roam freely.*

Q. Which has more protein, the meat of a cow or the meat of a bison?
A. *Bison meat has 30 percent more protein than beef, 70 percent less fat, and 59 percent less cholesterol. In fact, bison meat has less fat and cholesterol than chicken or fish.*

Q. Do bison moo?
A. *No, bison do not moo, but they do grunt.*

Q. Female bison give birth to one calf at a time; twins are rare. How much will a newborn calf weigh on average?
A. *40 to 50 pounds. A female bison can give birth every year if well nourished, into her mid-20s.*

The word "buffalo" might come from the French world "boeufs," meaning oxen or cattle.

> **A bison always has an escape route in mind. Should any perceived threat block that planned escape route, the animal immediately feels threatened and will charge. Tourists who would like a close-up photo of a bison would be well advised to keep this in mind.**

Q. How fast can a bison run when motivated?

A. *A bison can run 45 mph, which is a lot faster than a tourist can run.*

Q. Bison are discouraged from leaving Yellowstone for fear they may transmit brucellosis to area cattle. Brucellosis is a disease that can cause pregnant cattle to miscarry. How many instances are there on record of bison transferring brucellosis to cattle?

A) NONE   B) 1,500   C) 25,000

A. *A) None. Bison originally were brucellosis-free until Holsteins and Herefords were brought into their territory, carrying the disease with them. Brucellosis was first diagnosed in the Yellowstone bison herd in 1930. Ironically, the bison probably picked it up from the milk cows kept at the buffalo ranch prior to 1919.*

Q. During the especially harsh winter of 1996-97, what percent of Yellowstone's bison herd died?

A) 3 PERCENT   B) 12 PERCENT   C) 33 PERCENT

A. *C) About 33 percent. More than a thousand bison were killed as they searched for better forage outside park boundaries. Inside the park, another 1,800 died due to the hard winter, leaving less than a third of the herd alive—about 1,200 animals.*

Q. True or false: Bison do not get cancer.

A. *True, bison are thought to be the only mammal with immunity to cancer.*

The buffalo $10 bill was released in 1901, just as bison were on the brink of extinction.

> **In an average year, five Yellowstone tourists are injured by bison, making bison the park's most dangerous animal.**

Q. What is the hump on a bison's back for?

A. *The hump is made of muscle and helps power the heavy head as it swings back and forth like a steam shovel, moving aside deep snow to reach grass.*

Q. Which has a longer average life expectancy: cattle or bison?

A. *Bison can live 30 to 40 years; cattle live a maximum of 20 to 25 years.*

Q. An adult male bison weighing 2,000 pounds can do a standing jump over a fence how high?

A) 3 FEET
B) 6 FEET
C) 10 FEET

A. *B) Six feet high.*

> **"In our trip across the plains in 1862, after crossing the Red River of the North, buffaloes abounded everywhere. We thought the herds of 5,000, 10,000 or more, very large herds, until we got beyond the second crossing of the Cheyenne River, where the herds increased in size...I have no doubt that there were one million buffaloes in that herd."**
>
> *This quote was written by Nathaniel Langford about his trip west in 1862. In 1872, Langford became the first superintendent of Yellowstone National Park. By the time his term was over in 1877, bison were on the verge of oblivion.*

Bison can't lie down for long because their lungs begin to fill with fluid after 15 minutes.

Quote

Quest ™

Find the underlined words from this Paul Schullery quote about bison from his book "Mountain Time": "There is an old saying about the bull bison. If he raises his tail it means one of two things— charge or discharge." *When all the underlined words have been crossed out, the remaining letters will spell out William Hornaday's opinion of bison.*

```
A  B  U  F  F  B  A  L  O  W  I  L
A  L  L  S  U  U  R  V  I  V  E  W
H  B  E  I  R  L  E  C  T  E  T  D
H  E  O  B  A  L  E  H  H  R  S  I
S  T  R  U  A  T  D  A  I  E  N  S
N  G  E  S  T  L  T  R  N  H  E  C
A  E  R  W  O  O  U  G  G  T  B  H
E  L  D  L  I  T  E  E  S  I  R  A
M  A  S  E  S  I  A  R  S  L  L  R
Y  S  A  Y  I  N  G  O  F  R  E  G
E  Z  E  O  N  F  N  O  O  T  X  E
```

Hidden message:

" _ _____ ____ _____

_____ ___ ____ _____

_____ _____ _____

_____ __ ____ "

Answer on page 108

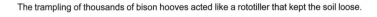

The trampling of thousands of bison hooves acted like a rototiller that kept the soil loose.

HISTORY

Q. The original inhabitants of the Yellowstone area were a band of natives called the Sheepeaters, so named because they occasionally hunted the bighorn sheep in the area and turned sheep horns into excellent hunting bows. They were said to be extremely shy, shunning all human contact, and rarely traveling more than a few miles from their home territory. The story of their shyness later tuned out to be a myth started by Park Superintendent Norris. Why did he make up this story?

A. *It was good publicity and spread the public image of Yellowstone as a wild and remote place. The tribe of about 400 Sheepeater Indians was later forcibly evicted from the park. They went to live with the Shoshones on the Wind River Reservation in Wyoming.*

Q. What was the Snake River named for?
    A) THE MANY SNAKES THAT LIVE IN THE AREA
    B) THE SERPENTINE SHAPE OF THE RIVER
    C) BASKET WEAVING DONE BY LOCAL TRIBES

A. *C) The Snake River was named because in Indian sign language the signal for the Shoshone tribe was a serpentine motion of the hand, with the fingers extended. This indicated the weaving of baskets and grass lodges by the Shoshone/Snake tribe. White men who didn't speak Indian sign language very fluently assumed the gesture referred to slithering snakes, and so the river—and the tribe—was named incorrectly.*

Q. What was the Shoshone name for the Yellowstone area?
    A) "WATER FLIES UP"
    B) "VALLEY OF MANY FAT BUFFALO"
    C) "WATER KEEPS ON COMING OUT"

A. *C) "Water keeps on coming out."*

In 1872—the year Yellowstone was declared the first national park—there were only 300 visitors.

Q. For years, trappers, hunters, and explorers had been coming out of Yellowstone telling tall tales of spouting water, stone forests, glass mountains, and boiling lakes, but these descriptions were largely dismissed as rumors. Finally, three prospectors from the Helena area decided to see what was up. The Cook-Folsom-Peterson expedition of 1869 was the first organized exploration of the area that later became Yellowstone. These men spent 36 days exploring and confirmed all the wild tales. Folsom wrote an account of their journey and submitted it to magazine after magazine, but it was roundly rejected until finally being published by *Western Monthly*. Why was his article turned down so often?

A. *Editors thought the account was so fantastic it could not possibly be true.*

Q. Great Fountain Geyser in the Lower Geyser Basin, which erupts to the height of 150 feet, was the first geyser to be scientifically observed. In 1869 the Cook-Folsom-Peterson party arrived in the area just in time to see the eruption. After hearing so many wild tales from people like Jim Bridger and John Colter, finally the truth was evident. What was their reaction?

A) THEY TURNED AND FLED IN FRIGHT

B) THEY APPROACHED TOO CLOSELY AND WERE SCALDED

C) THEY SCREAMED AND SHOUTED

A. *C) Cook described their reaction this way: "We could not contain our enthusiasm; with one accord we all took off our hats and yelled with all our might."*

"Judge, then, of our astonishment on entering this basin, to see at no great distance before us an immense body of sparkling water, projected suddenly and with terrific force into the air to the height of over one hundred feet. We had found a real geyser!" *Nathaniel Langford, upon meeting Old Faithful*

It its first 62 years as a park, Yellowstone had 3 million visitors.

Q. Railroad magnate Jay Cooke wanted to run a railroad westward but he needed to be sure there were attractions that would attract tourist traffic as well as commercial traffic. He was interested in Folsom's account of the Yellowstone area and hired Nathaniel P. Langford to explore the area. Langford teamed up with Henry Washburn, who was Montana Territory's surveyor general; journalist Cornelius Hedges; an unemployed tax collector named Truman Everts; and First Lieutenant Gustavus Doane, who led the military contingent of the expedition. Which member of this 1871 expedition was later appointed the first superintendent of the new national park?

A. *Nathaniel P. Langford.*

Q. Which member of this expedition is generally credited with being the first person to suggest the area should be set aside as a national park?

A. *Cornelius Hedges, a journalist, is generally credited with being the first person to make the suggestion. The discussion allegedly took place around a campfire one night on the trip, and a nearby peak was named National Park Mountain in honor of the idea. This episode may be myth, but it makes a good story.*

Q. The reports written by Washburn encouraged Dr. Ferdinand Hayden, a U.S. Geological Survey geologist, to explore the park in 1872. Hayden's expedition was the first that was sponsored and paid for by the U.S. government. Hayden took along geologists, zoologists, and botanists. Yet, it was his crucial decision to take along Thomas Moran and William Henry Jackson that turned the tide in favor of creating a national park. Why were Moran and Jackson so critical to the success of the passage of the congressional bill that protected the area?

A. *Jackson was an artist and Moran was a photographer. Their pictures were the first the public had ever seen of the area, and it allowed people (especially the congressmen who were shortly to vote on the issue) to believe all the stories they had heard.*

Today, more than 3 million visitors come to Yellowstone every single year.

The Washburn expedition was no piece of cake. Some of the men got sick, possibly from toxic water or noxious fumes, or from eating poorly canned peaches. Lt. Doane had an injured thumb that got so badly infected he was unable to keep his journal and often was unable to sleep. Nathaniel Langford got tangled in the rope of a horse and dragged over a log. Later he nearly scalded himself in a hot spring and his horse broke through a thin crust and scalded its legs in hot mud. Everts got hopelessly lost and nearly starved to death. Washburn got sick while searching for Everts and died of pneumonia a few months later. Yet, because these were reliable people who were well known, their stories of the wonders of the area were believed. Because of their journey, interest in preserving the area spread like wildfire.

Q. Thomas Moran was working for the popular *Scribner's Magazine* as an illustrator when the magazine published Langford's account of his trip to the area. Moran illustrated the article without ever having seen the park. Jay Cooke of the Northern Pacific Railroad paved the way for Moran to accompany Hayden's survey because he wanted to build a profitable railroad line to Yellowstone and knew that publicity was essential to having the area set aside as a park. Moran returned from the trip and painted a masterpiece called "Grand Cañon of the Yellowstone" that created a sensation and launched his career. How big was the painting?

A) 3 FEET BY 3 FEET   B) 6 FEET BY 7 FEET   C) 12 FEET BY 7 FEET

A. *C) Twelve feet wide and seven feet tall. Congress purchased the painting, and it was one of the first landscape paintings to grace the walls of the House of Representatives.*

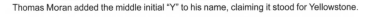

Thomas Moran added the middle initial "Y" to his name, claiming it stood for Yellowstone.

Q. What glaring inaccuracy appears in Moran's famous painting?

A. *The painting, depicting the Grand Canyon from what today is called Artist's Point, shows the Teton Mountains on the horizon even though in reality you cannot see the Tetons from there. Moran took a variety of artistic liberties with the painting.*

Q. Hayden's findings, including photos, sketches, and physical specimens, were laid before Congress in 1872 and Congress quickly passed legislation establishing the world's first national park. Why was Congress in such a hurry?

A. *Because the Homestead Act, passed in 1862, was sending a flood of pioneers to the West to stake homestead claims. No one wanted private citizens claiming the features of the park.*

> **First Lieutenant Gustavus Doane led a futile winter exploration of the area. During the trip, the party was attempting to descend the Heart River when their boat developed leaks. They threw water on the cracks. The water froze immediately, sealing the cracks.**

Q. Yellowstone became the first national park in 1872, but what area became the second national park, after the concept of national parks became known as "America's Best Idea?"

A. *The second national park was Sequoia, followed by Yosemite, which were both established in 1890, followed by Mount Rainier in 1899, Glacier in 1910, Rocky Mountain in 1915, and Grand Canyon in 1919.*

Nathanial P. Langford later claimed his first two initials stood for "National Park" Langford.

Q. William Henry Jackson brought the world its first views of Yellowstone through his photographs, but he was also a talented artist. In 1935, the National Park Service asked him to produce a series of paintings commemorating the Hayden Expedition, and he complied. How old was he at the time of this request?

A. *92, and he was 95 when they were finished. In the time it took him to complete these paintings, he also completed another six similar canvases, as well as 40 watercolors. He died at the age of 99. His painting entitled "First Official Exploration of the Yellowstone, Wyoming Region," depicting members of the Hayden party watching Old Faithful, hangs in the Department of the Interior. Jackson painted himself in the picture.*

Q. Why were leaders in the Montana Territory so anxious to see Yellowstone preserved as a national park?

A. *They didn't want neighboring Wyoming Territory to claim the park as its very own attraction.*

Q. What percent of Yellowstone is in Wyoming?

A. *96 percent, and 3 percent in Montana and 1 percent in Idaho.*

Q. Cooke City was named for Jay Cooke, president of the Northern Pacific Railroad. Townsfolk hoped the flattery would convince Cooke to run a railroad to their isolated town to haul mining products to market. Did the ploy work?

A. *No, in fact, Jay Cooke never visited Cooke City.*

> **Tower Fall was named by a member of the Washburn-Langford-Doane expedition after his sweetheart, Miss Tower. They had agreed not to name anything after themselves or their friends and this was a sneaky way to do it. Another member of the party wanted to name a waterfall Minaret after his girlfriend, Minnie Rhett, but that was rejected as too transparent.**

When Thomas Moran died at age 89 in 1926, the unfinished canvas on his easel...

Q. When Yellowstone was made a national park in 1872, what was the park's annual operating budget allotted by Congress?
A) $0   B) $10,000 ANNUALLY   C) $100,000 ANNUALLY

A. *A) No money was provided. There were so many opponents to the idea of the park that this was the only way to silence them.*

Q. Nathaniel P. Langford was appointed the first superintendent of the park, but he served for no pay because the park had no budget. Therefore, he made his living in Helena. How often did he visit the park during his five-year term as head administrator?
A) 3   B) 17   C) 26

A. *A) Three times.*

> **Philetus W. Norris was the second superintendent of Yellowstone and the first to receive a federal salary for his work. He served from 1877-1882. He wrote one of the first guidebooks to Yellowstone. It was entitled, *Calumet of the Coteau and Other Poetical Legends of the Border, Also a Glossary of Indian Names, Words, and Western Provincialisms, Together with a Guide-Book of the Yellowstone National Park*. It was published in 1883 and included a lot of his poetry.**

Q. What year did the first wheeled vehicle—a stagecoach—first enter the park?

A. August 30, 1878. It made it all the way to Old Faithful on rutted pathways full of stumps. Because Congress had not budgeted any money for Yellowstone, Superintendent Langford was unable to build many roads. When Superintendent Norris took over in 1878, he convinced Congress to allocate money to the park, and the number of roads increased from 32 miles to 153 miles during his term.

...at his studio in Long Island depicted Tower Fall in Yellowstone.

Q. What year was the Grand Loop completed, making it possible to see most of Yellowstone's major sites from a single figure-8 road system?

A. *1905.*

Q. Photographer F. Jay Haynes arrived in Yellowstone in 1881 and was named official park photographer in 1883. He ran a series of photo shops in the park and also had interests in the stage lines and the first motorcar company to operate in the park. He published guidebooks and sold innumerable postcards. What was unique about Haynes's darkroom?

A. *For many years, Haynes's darkroom was located in a railroad car so he could travel around the U.S. taking pictures for the railroad and developing them on the spot.*

Q. In the years before hotels, restaurants, and tour buses, visitors took their food with them or caught it along the way. The act of Congress that set aside Yellowstone as a park prohibited the "wanton destruction of the fish and game found within said park, and against their capture or destruction for the purposes of merchandise or profit," but this did not prevent people from killing far more animals than they needed to feed themselves as they traveled through the park. In what year were laws passed in Congress prohibiting both sport hunting and subsistence hunting in the park?

A) 1873   B) 1883   C) 1893

A. *B) 1883.*

"All persons traveling through the park from October 1 to June 1 should be regarded with suspicion." *-from "Rules, Regulations, and Instructions for the information and guidance of officers and enlisted men of the U.S. Army, and of the Scouts doing duty in the Yellowstone National Park" a guidebook for park personnel published in 1907.*

General Washburn named Old Faithful and it has erupted faithfully ever since.

Q. Because there was no money for law enforcement or administration, early park tourists ran wild. With wildlife being killed, travertine terraces being splintered, and petrified forests being carried away, something had to be done. In what year was the Army sent in to protect the park from thievery, vandalism, and poaching?

    A) 1874   B) 1882   C) 1886

A. *C) 1886. The Army's headquarters were at Mammoth, although from 1891 through 1918 it was called Fort Yellowstone. There's a lot of nice architecture in Mammoth because when it was Fort Yellowstone, it received more foreign visitors than any other army post with the possible exception of West Point. The army barracks are now employee housing.*

Q. In 1916, President Woodrow Wilson signed the bill forming the National Park Service. The Army moved out of Yellowstone and park rangers moved in. What event caused this shift?

A. *Because soldiers were needed to fight World War I and there was no one left to guard the park.*

> **A businessman named Stephen Mather, following a visit to Yosemite, wrote to Interior Secretary Franklin Lane in 1914 to complain about the bad conditions in the national parks: trails were impassable; cattle roamed freely; timber companies continued to cut lumber within boundaries. Because Lane and Mather had been classmates at the University of California, the Interior Secretary sent a short reply: "Dear Steve, if you don't like the way the national parks are being run, come on down to Washington and run them yourself." Mather did. In 1915 he became Lane's assistant in charge of national parks. When President Wilson established the National Park Service in 1916, Mather became its first director.**

Grant Village is named after Pres. Grant who signed the legislation establishing the park.

Q. The town of Gardiner and the Gardner River are named after trapper and trader Johnson Gardner, who lived nearby. Why is the town spelled one way and the river spelled another way?

A. *Because when explorer Jim Bridger was describing landmarks to a mapmaker, his Virginia drawl put an extra syllable into the word.*

Q. Which was the first lodge ever built in the park?

A. *Mammoth Hot Springs Hotel, opening in 1883. It was torn down in 1936 and a new complex was built.*

Q. Which of the lodges in the park is the oldest lodge still in use?
   A) LAKE HOTEL
   B) OLD FAITHFUL INN
   C) MAMMOTH HOTEL

A. *A) Lake Hotel is the oldest hotel still in use in the park. It was built with Northern Pacific Railroad money between 1889 and 1891. It was completely remodeled in the mid-1980s and restored to its original glory. It's the longest wooden hotel in the world at 890 feet long.*

Q. During stagecoach days, even the hardiest of visitors could travel only 20 miles a day, so lodgings were built 20 miles apart. They were located at Mammoth Hot Springs, Fountain Paint Pots, Old Faithful, Yellowstone Lake, and the Grand Canyon. Today, how many of these original lodges remain?
   A) NONE   B) TWO   C) FOUR

A. *B) Only two: Old Faithful Inn and Lake Hotel. Many lodges were removed after cars became common in the park because it was so much easier to get around.*

Q. Old Faithful Inn was completed in 1904 at a total cost of $140,000 (not including the $25,000 budgeted for furnishings). How much would $140,000 be worth in today's dollars?

A. *Adjusted for inflation, about $2.7 million.*

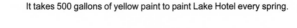

It takes 500 gallons of yellow paint to paint Lake Hotel every spring.

Q. Bill Scales was winter keeper at Lake Hotel in the spring of 1903 when President Theodore Roosevelt and his party came to the park for two weeks of camping. Scales refused to open the closed and shuttered hotel for the president. When he was later asked to account for his ungracious behavior, what was his reply?

A. *Scales said that the honor of meeting the president wasn't worth the hassle of cleaning up the mess his crowd would make.*

Q. In 1902, automobiles were illegal in the park. But one day Henry G. Merry defied this rule and jubilantly drove his brand new Winton auto into the park. He roared past a group of mounted cavalry at a breakneck speed of 25 mph, sending their horses into a frenzy. The outraged soldiers pursued the car, caught up with it where it had been slowed by a steep grade, lassoed the vehicle, hog-tied the car, and hauled the miscreant driver to the park administrator for punishment. Merry admitted his guilt and accepted the punishment. What was the punishment?

A) TEN DAYS IN THE CLINK

B) $25 FINE

C) GIVING THE CURIOUS PARK ADMINISTRATOR A RIDE IN HIS NEWFANGLED WINTON AUTOMOBILE.

A. *C) Merry had to give the administrator a ride.*

Q. Mount Rainier was the first National Park to admit cars in 1908, followed by General Grant National Park in 1910, Crater Lake in 1911, Glacier in 1912, and Yosemite and Sequoia in 1913. Yellowstone was opened to cars in 1915. Why was Yellowstone so late in allowing automobile traffic?

A. *Because concessionaire Harry Child had a lot of money tied up in the Yellowstone stagecoach business and he had a lot of influence with the Interior Department. The railroads also lobbied against vehicle traffic in order to protect their profits.*

Old Faithful Inn opened in 1904, more than a decade before the first cars arrived.

Q. How much were admission rates for vehicles in 1915?
A) 50 CENTS PER CAR   B) $2 PER CAR   C) $5 PER CAR

A. *C) $5 for single passenger cars; $7.50 for five-passenger cars, and $10 for seven passenger cars. That's a steep price; adjusted for today's dollars, $5 would be equal to $93.*

Q. When the park allowed autos in 1915, all cars had to stop at established checkpoints where the drivers would hand over their park passes to an attendant, who would note the time of day and write it down on the pass. Attendants knew exactly how long it would take to travel to the next checkpoint at park speed limits. If the driver arrived at the next checkpoint too quickly, he would be fined for speeding. The fines were 50 cents per minute if the driver was five minutes too early and $1 per minute for the next 20 minutes too early. How much was the fine for being more than 25 minutes early?

A. *$25 or ejection from the park—or both.*

> The original road between **Old Faithful and West Thumb**, built in 1891, was considerably more crooked than the current road. One stretch of the road was dubbed **Corkscrew Hill** because it was "so crooked that you pass one place three times before you get by it, and then meet yourself on the road coming back," according to a guidebook written in 1928. In 1938 a new, improved road was installed, straightening out many of the turns.

Corkscrew Hill?
I know that road
like the back
of my hand...

On a typical summer day there is one patrol ranger for every 1,000 visitors in the park.

Q. Most of the roads were graveled before 1920; they were oiled before 1930; and paving began in 1936. When was the pavement on the final stretch of road—from West Thumb to Old Faithful—completed?

A. *1946.*

Q. What led to Charles Hamilton's great success as a park concessionaire in Yellowstone?

A. *Hamilton correctly guessed that automobiles would be the wave of the future, and he invested in gas stations, lunch counters, and souvenir shops that catered to the motoring crowd.*

Around the turn of the century, summer employee Charles Hamilton teamed up with Huntley Child, the son of the park superintendent. They stole a load of dynamite and set it off at Mammoth to celebrate the 4th of July. Their planned celebration backfired, however, when the force of the explosion shattered every single window in the vicinity. Child, being the son of the boss, got off scot-free, but Charles Hamilton was banished from the park for a time. In 1915, long after the smoke settled and the windows were repaired, Charles Hamilton returned to the park when Huntley Child sent him word that the store located at Old Faithful was up for sale due to the death of the previous owner. Charles Hamilton bought the business without hesitation and used it to launch a successful chain of concession stores that catered to tourists throughout the park for decades.

It's estimated that one-third of Americans will see Yellowstone in their lifetimes.

Q. In 1924 Charles Hamilton began construction on a new store at Yellowstone Lake. He chose a site but then found that the access road would have to go over the top of the lone grave of some unknown, long forgotten person—or else it would cost a huge amount of money to detour the road around the grave. After considering the situation at length, what did Hamilton do to solve the problem?

A. *Hamilton picked up the tombstone and moved it a short distance away, erected a picket fence around it, placed some memorial flowers on top, and proceeded with the road as planned, leaving the body where it was. Some say a ghost wanders the area, searching for its missing tombstone.*

Q. Park Superintendent Horace Albright hired the park's first ranger in 1919. How long before the park's first female ranger was hired?

A) THAT SAME YEAR   B) TEN YEARS   C) FIFTY YEARS

A. *A) That same year. In 1919 Isabel Basset Wasson became a ranger and her duties included giving talks at hotels and starting a museum. She had a degree in geology. Isabel was the second ranger hired in Yellowstone.*

Q. In 1921 Marguerite Lindsley became the second female ranger in the park and guided walks through Mammoth Hot Springs. By 1926 four more women were on the staff. Then, Chief Inspector J.F. Gartland reported to the Secretary of the Interior that women should not be serving as rangers. An order came down from Washington, D.C., not to hire any more women as rangers or naturalists. When Herma Alberston Baggley resigned her position in 1933, approximately how long was it before another woman filled a ranger position in Yellowstone?

A) TEN YEARS   B) TWENTY YEARS   C) THIRTY YEARS

A. *C) Thirty years.*

The average visitor stays in the park a day and a half.

Q. Edmund Rogers took over as superintendent of the park in 1936 and served longer than any other superintendent. How long did he serve?

A. *20 years. In 1957 he left Yellowstone to become special assistant to the National Park Service director.*

Q. Why are Yellowstone's concessionaire employees commonly referred to as "savages?"

A. *The term dates back to 1920 when writer and tourist Elizabeth Frazer wrote an article about the park in the* Saturday Evening Post: *"They [the drivers escorting tourists through the park] used to go hell-for-leather round those narrow mountain curves in order to hear the dudes and tourist ladies screech. So we got to calling them savages because they were such a raw bunch."*

> **August 11, 1921 Ora Phillips and W.C. Brooks of Nebraska crashed their plane into the shallow shore of Yellowstone Lake. According to the *Denver Post* on August 12, 1921, "This was the first plane to land within the park boundary. Congress has not made any regulations relevant to the entrance of the flying craft and park officials are at a loss as to how to collect entrance fees for it."**

Q. What man who later became president of the United States worked as a seasonal employee in the park in 1936?

A) Richard Nixon   B) Lyndon Johnson   C) Gerald Ford

A. *C) Gerald Ford. Years later his son Jack was also a summer employee.*

90 percent of tourists visit the park between June and August.

YELLOWSTONE TRIVIA   102

Q. What famous movie star was a tour guide in Yellowstone for four summers before going to Hollywood and becoming a leading man?
A) GARY COOPER   B) CARY GRANT   C) ROCK HUDSON

A. *A) Gary Cooper was a "gear jammer" tour guide.*

Q. What years recorded the largest leap in attendance at the park?
A) 1872-1874, WHEN THE PARK WAS FIRST ESTABLISHED
B) 1915-1917, WHEN CARS WERE FIRST ALLOWED
C) 1945-1947, WHEN WORLD WAR II ENDED

A. *C) 1945-1947, when World War II ended. In 1872, the year the park was established, there were only 300 visitors. There were fewer than 10,000 visitors in the next ten years. Attendance got a big boost when cars were allowed in the park in 1915 and increased steadily over the years. However, business got so bad during World War II that in 1942 the park concession company asked the National Park Service to close the park altogether.*

Q. When the concessionaire asked the National Park Service to close the park due to poor attendance, was the request honored?

A. *No, but business operations in the park were scaled way back in 1943. In 1944, only 85,350 visitors came to the park. But in 1945 the war was over, soldiers were home, and gas rationing ceased. Some 178,300 visitors came that year. When gas rationing ended on August 13, 1945, tourists flooded back in record numbers, completely overwhelming the few employees that were on hand at the time. In 1947, 923,000 people visited the park.*

Q. In 1918 the film *Cupid Angling* starring Mary Pickford and Douglas Fairbanks was filmed partially in Yellowstone. What was unusual about this early film?

A. Cupid Angling *was the first full-length movie shot in color.*

More than 3 million people visit every year -- that's about six times the population of Wyoming.

Q. What 1998 movie filmed in Yellowstone featured Paul Walker and Steve Van Wormer as two surfer dudes who end up as Yellowstone park rangers assigned to fight an overpopulation of prairie dogs while battling an evil ex-ranger who is trying to steal Old Faithful?

A. *Meet the Deedles.*

Q. Which of the Star Trek movies featured scenes from Yellowstone as a stand-in for the planet Vulcan?

A. *The original* Star Trek: The Motion Picture *featured Mammoth Hot Springs as the planet Vulcan.*

Q. What 1980 movie partially filmed in Yellowstone starred Charlton Heston and Brian Keith as trappers in a realistic portrayal of life in 1838?

A. *The Mountain Men.*

Presidential Tourists

* President Chester Arthur caught 103 pounds of trout when he visited the park in 1883.
* President Harding hand-fed snacks to bears along the road when he visited the park in 1923, shortly before his death. (His death was not related to the bears.)
* President Kennedy visited Yellowstone two months before he was shot.
* President Jimmy Carter visited Yellowstone in 1978.
* President Bill Clinton, wife Hillary, and daughter Chelsea visited the park in 1996.

Canada was the second country to set aside a national park: Banff in 1885.

Quote Quest™

Find all the underlined words from this quote by Robin Winks, Chairman, National Park Service Advisory Board: "The <u>true test</u> of the <u>nature</u> of <u>national character</u> is in <u>what people choose</u>, by a <u>conscious act</u>, in the <u>face</u> of <u>contending choices</u>, to <u>preserve</u>." *When all the underlined words have been crossed out, the remaining letters will spell out a related quote by Charles Lindbergh.*

```
T I N N A T U R E C W W I
C C H O I C E S L H D E P
A R N E S S I S A A E N R
S S E N T H E T M R I G E
U R A C A L E O F A L N S
O I F E E T A N D C B I E
I E H U I N I D I T T D R
C E O R U R S O C E I N V
S E S T N T I T N R F E E
N I C O A C S C O A C T M
O E L P O E P P L A L N I
C S H M T H E N F T S O F
A D E T O T C R I V I C A
```

Hidden message:

"__ _____ _ _____ ___

_____ __ ____ ___ ____ _

__ ___ _____

_____ ___ ____ __

"

_____

Answer on page 109

There are 388 units in the National Park system today.

DEATH IN
YELLOWSTONE

❖

Q. Which has been responsible for more deaths in Yellowstone: grizzly bears or hot springs?

A. *Hot springs have killed far more people than bears. After all, there are around 10,000 thermal features in the park, but only about 350 grizzly bears.*

Q. How many people have been killed by bears in the park?
   A) 5   B) 22   C) 112

A. *A) Five, compared to 20 people who have died in hot springs.*

Q. Of the 20 deaths from hot springs, what percentage have been children?
   A) ONE-TENTH   B) ONE-THIRD   C) ONE-HALF

A. *B) One-third.*

Q. How many people have been killed by bison in the history of the park?
   A) 2   B) 17   C) 56

A. *Two, making it the second most deadly animal.*

Q. Cars were first allowed in the park on August 1st of 1915. How long before the first automobile fatality occurred?
   A) ONE MONTH   B) ONE YEAR   C) ONE DECADE

A. *A) One month. On September 3, 1915, Sarah Edith Higgins, a 49-year-old woman from Helena, fractured her skull when the Maxwell in which she was riding skidded on a slick road and crashed down a 60-foot embankment between Tower Junction and Mammoth.*

By 1956, 98.7% of visitors came to the park in cars.

Q. What kills the most people in Yellowstone?

A. *The top killers in the park are, in order: car crashes, illness, drowning, and falls.*

Q. On July 14, 1924, Mr. And Mrs. Earl Dunn of Minneapolis were touring the park in their car. Somehow while backing out of their parking space at the rim of the Grand Canyon of the Yellowstone, Mr. Dunn backed right over the lip of the canyon. Perhaps he hit the gas instead of the brake. How far did the car freefall before hitting a cliff wall?

A) 100 FEET   B) 500 FEET   C) 800 FEET

A. *C) The car fell 800 feet before striking a cliff and tumbling end-over-end for another 200 feet, where it came to rest next to the river.*

Q. Where do the majority of drownings occur in Yellowstone?

A. *About 40 percent of the drownings happen in Yellowstone Lake. Most involve small boats or canoes that overturn in sudden storms.*

Q. On average in the summer, the water temperature in Yellowstone Lake is 41°F. What is the average survival time in water this cold?

A) 6 MINUTES   B) 30 MINUTES   C) 2 HOURS

A. *B) 30 minutes.*

Q. Water hemlock is one of the most poisonous plants in the world. When a popular park naturalist named Charles Phillips ate some for supper in 1927, thinking it harmless, he died the next day. Where will you find Phillip's Caldron, named in his honor?

A. *In Norris Geyser Basin.*

> **Lee Whittlesey, in his book *Death In Yellowstone: Accidents and Foolhardiness in the First National Park*, reminds us to be careful and respectful of the park's wildness, saying, "Not only can it bite us, indeed, it can devour us."**

Yellowstone became the world's first national park in 1872...

PUZZLE ANSWERS

Quote Quest Pg. 16

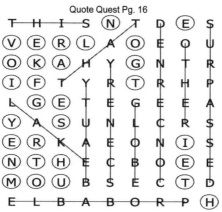

```
T  H  I  S  (N) T  D  (E) S
(V)(E)(R)(L)(A)(O) E  O  U
(O)(K)(A)(H) Y (G) N  T  R
(I)(F) T  Y  R (T) R  H  P
 L (G)(E) T  E  G  E  E  A
(Y)(A)(S) U  N  L  C  R  S
(E)(R)(K) A  E  O  N (I) S
(N)(T)(H) E  C  B  O (E) E
(M)(O)(U) B  S  E  C (T) D
 E  L  B  A  B  O  R  P (H)
```

Hidden message: "Never look a gift geyser in the mouth." -Rudyard Kipling

Quote Quest Pg. 39

```
(A)(P)(I) T (C)(T)(U)(R)(E)(O)(F)(W) H (O)
(N)(D)(H) W (S)(E)(H)(E)(L)(L)(R)(A)(E)(N)
(D)(I)(Ø) L  T (S)(T)(A)(H)(T)(H)(O)(R) G
 S (N)(D) A  I  N (R)(R) F  I  R  E  E  O
 S (O)(E) C  T (I)(R)(S)(S)(I)(T)(U)(A) R
 B (T)(P) I  C  A (H)(O)(T)(P)(O)(T)(S) G
 O (G)(P) T  H (E)(W)(D)(E)(H)(I)(N) E
 U (N)(A) R  E  N  N (A)(I)(T)(A)(U)(N) S
 N (I)(C) E  R  U (I)(E) R  L  W  M  E  O
 D (D)(E) V  Y (O)(U)(A) V  T  D (E)(E) P
 O (N) T (S)(I) M  E  T (S)(A) M (I)(R) O
(N)(A) I (B)(E)(T)(W)(D)(E)(E)(E)(E)(N) E
(H)(T)(H)(A)(E)(A)(I)(V)(D)(E)(N)(H)(A)(N)
(D) S  W (H)(R)(M)(E)(L)(L) E  C  A  L  P
```

Hidden message: "A picture of wonder and horror, situated in a unique position between heaven and hell." (Anonymous)

Acrostic Pg. 25

Year
Erupt
Lava
Lake
Oak
Washburn
Specimen Ridge
Tokyo
Obsidian
Nebraska
Erode

Word Scramble Pg. 26

Animals
trumpeter swan
osprey
cougar
wolves
cutthroat trout
grizzly
antelope
bighorn sheep
moose
bison
coyote
Things
obsidian
granite
rhyolite
petrified forest
fumaroles
geyserite
travertine
lodgepole pine
Places
Mammoth
Norris
Old Faithful

...Today there are more than 1,500 national parks and preserves worldwide.

Quote Quest Pg. 44

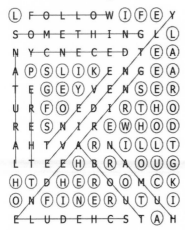

Hidden message: "Life leaps like a geyser for those who drill through the rock of inertia." -Alexis Carrel

Quote Quest Pg. 70

Hidden message: "Oh give me a home where the buffalo roam, and I'll show you a house with a really messy kitchen!"

Quote Quest Pg. 80

Hidden message: "It is said that you can herd a buffalo anywhere it wants to go." -anonymous

Quote Quest Pg. 86

Hidden message: "A buffalo will survive where the best range steer would literally freeze on foot." -William Hornaday

---

1,752,345 vehicles drove through the park in 2005, carrying more than 3 million people...

Quote Quest Pg. 104

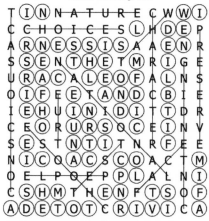

Hidden message: "In wilderness I sense the miracle of life and behind it our scientific accomplishments fade to trivia." -Charles Lindbergh

Crossword Solution, Pg. 15

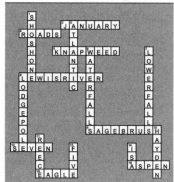

Crossword Solution, Pg. 40

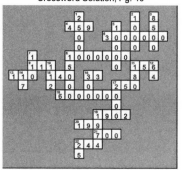

...5,125 of those 1.7 million vehicles were busses, both school and tour busses.

Index

The Yellowstone hot spot is the largest known center of active volcanism on the planet.

Geologists are able to identify volcanic rocks from about 100 different explosions.

Water coming up in geysers or springs may have fallen as rain or snow up to 500 years ago.

If spray from geysers hits your glasses, binoculars, or camera, it will leave permanent spots.

Five Surprising Facts About Montana:
1. The only states with more pick-up trucks per capita than
   Montana are North and South Dakota.
2. More tourists come to Montana from California than from
   any other state, followed by Washington and Texas.
3. There are around 250 miles of streets in Butte- and over
   2,500 miles of underground mining tunnels.
4. It would take about 13 hours at maximum capacity of
   72,000 people per hour to give every Montana resident a
   lift in the state's 65 ski lifts.
5. There are three times as many cows as humans in Montana.

In 1888, a park guidebook referred to Hazle Lake near Norris Geyser Basin...

...accidentally misspelling Hazel. The lake has been misspelled ever since.

TERRIFIC BOOKS ABOUT YELLOWSTONE

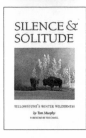